OFF ROAD LEADERSHIP
A GUIDE FOR YOUNG LEADERS AND THOSE
WHO MENTOR THEM

RICK OLMSTEAD

PRAISE FOR OFF ROAD LEADERSHIP

"You hold in your hands a true treasure! The older I get, the more I hear from young leaders is their heart-cry for senior, more experienced leaders to mentor them with authenticity and transparency in preparation for navigating the realities of a life of leadership. Rick Olmstead, a respected pastor, leader of 'Generation Now' and the 'Global 4/14 Window Movement' does just that, both in his life and in the pages of this book. Imagine sitting around a campfire with a wise and encouraging leader as conversations flow through a lifetime of his ups and downs in leadership. I've had that privilege with my dear friend Rick over the years, and have no doubt you will too."

Dr. Wess Stafford
President Emeritus, Compassion International,
Board of Awana, 4/14 Window Movement
Author of *Too Small to Ignore* and
Just a Minute: *In the Heart of a Child*

"The first time I met Rick, I knew I would like this guy. He's real, he's raw, and he shares my love for pastors. I'm so glad he wrote this book. We need to learn from men who live well and finish strong. I would encourage you to take an "off-road" journey with Rick. You'll be better for it."

Greg Surratt
Founding Pastor of Seacoast Church,
and ARC Network of Churches

"With wisdom and transparency Rick Olmstead pulls back the curtain to explore the things that matter most in pastoral ministry (and life in general). If you are an emerging leader, or a mentor to one, I encourage you to both read and reflect on the important life lessons contained in the book."

Larry Osborne
Former Lead Pastor and present Teaching Pastor at
North Coast Church in Vista, California
Author of *Sticky Teams, Accidental Pharisees,
Lead Like a Shepherd, Thriving in Babylon*

"Countless books have been written on the subject of leadership, with authors often resorting to overused slogans and outdated illustrations. Rick Olmstead's book, Off Road: Leadership for a Now Generation, offers a fresh approach to a timeless topic. This book will inspire you -- and stretch you -- to be the leader God destined you to be."

Hal Donaldson
President, Convoy of Hope
Author of *Disruptive Compassion, Your Next 24 hours*

"Off Road beautifully describes a vision for intergenerational leadership, a call for older and newer leaders to cultivate symbiotic relationships that are exponentially more effective in Kingdom ministry. This book is a generous gift of one pastor's hard-won wisdom from decades spent serving the Lord and the church. Rick has been an incredible gift in my life, and I am grateful that his life's lessons are now available for the enrichment of generations to come."

Jay Pathak
National Director of VineyardUSA,
Founding Pastor of Mile High Vineyard Church
Author of *The Art of Neighboring*

In "*Off Road: Leadership for a New Generation*, Rick extends his voice to this emerging generation of young leaders and offers principles critical for navigating uncharted waters for today's uncertain times. I wholeheartedly recommend this book to any young leader stepping into ministry and those who mentor them."

Dr. Luis Bush
Author, Missionary, Strategist and Catalyst
Launched Trans World, 10/40 Window,
4/14 Window, and AD2000 Movements

"It would be hard to find a more spiritually sensitive or emotionally intelligent guide for young leaders in ministry than Rick. I've had the privilege of knowing Rick and Becky for several years. Many ministry leaders would be struck by their professional accomplishments including planting a great church, providing denominational leadership for children and youth ministry, and most recently providing vision and voice for the global 4/14 movement. But their greatest gift to the kingdom is the tenderness and spiritual sensitivity of their hearts."

Chad Causey, PhD
Chief Strategy Officer, OneHope Inc.
Chair of The Bob and Hazel Hoskins School of Mission,
Southeastern University

"Leadership with fresh eyes" has been my experience with Rick. He has inspired me to be a leader with a father's heart and a father's eyes. On his first visit to Watoto, he spoke to our young adults 'History Makers' event inspiring them as a father who didn't have one himself. This is a book for the NOW generation of leaders who want to have a significant kingdom impact."

Julius Rwotlonyo
Global 4/14 Movement, Lead Pastor, Watoto Church, Uganda

"Rick's ministry experience, wisdom, and longevity, prove a valuable resource for anyone, but especially for emerging leaders like me. Through biblical example, personal story, and spiritual maturity, Rick guides you on a variety of leadership topics to encourage you for the long haul. His friendship and mentoring meant so much to me as a young leader and I'm thankful many more will receive the same."

Jeff Faust
Lead Pastor of Vineyard Church of the Rockies

"Rick Olmstead's book *Off Road Leadership* is a valuable resource for leaders both young and old! With decades of experience and expertise, Rick generously shares wisdom, lessons learned, and counsel that will help young leaders navigate the challenges and complexities of leadership. Older leaders will find this book helpful as they guide, coach, and release a new generation of leaders. This book is like a reference guide for leadership, full of practical wisdom and inspiring stories."

Julie Yoder
Senior Pastor, Regional Overseer Vineyard USA

"*Off Road* is a living testimony of a true servant leader who is opening his heart and his life story so we might know what God can do through someone who says Yes to Him. This book a must read for every leader, especially young leaders. I want to give a copy to each one of mine. Pastor Rick comes with authentic authority, because it's biblically based and a life experience of one the most fruitful servant leaders in our generation. Thank you Pastor Rick for sharing your amazing God story and insights for a new generation of young leaders."

Afeef Halasah
Founder & Director of the A.F.T.A. Church Planting Movement

Scripture quotations marked (NIV) are taken from the Holy Bible, New International Version®, NIV®. Copyright © 1973, 1978, 1984, 2011 by Biblica, Inc.™ Used by permission of Zondervan. All rights reserved worldwide. www.zondervan.comThe "NIV" and "New International Version" are trademarks registered in the United States Patent and Trademark Office by Biblica, Inc.™

Scripture quotations marked (NLT) are from the Holy Bible, New Living Translation, © 1996, 2004, 2015 by Tyndale House Foundation. Used by permission of Tyndale House Publishers, Inc., Carol Stream, Illinois 60188. All rights reserved.

© 2023 Rick Olmstead

All rights reserved.

Published by Generation Now.

Cover design by Geoff Olmstead

Interior design by Green E-Books

For additional information please visit rickolmstead.org.

OFF ROAD LEADERSHIP
A GUIDE FOR YOUNG LEADERS AND THOSE WHO MENTOR THEM

To my wife Becky, and twin sons Greg and Geoff.

We have truly been a family on-mission. Going together on all those ministry trips was life changing for all of us and gave us great family memories. Trips to England, Scotland, Germany, Austria, Czech Republic, Hungary, Russia, Australia and Jordan bonded us together in special ways. Thank you for your patience, support and sacrifice over the years. I am more grateful and proud of you than any book that could ever be written. Your fingerprints are everywhere in this book but even more in my heart and life.

ACKNOWLEDGMENTS

I once read that if you ever see turtles on top of a fence you can be certain that they did not get there by themselves. I could not be where I am today without those who have stood by me and encouraged me throughout the years.

- To John Wimber who taught me so much about leadership and opened the door to endless opportunities to grow as a leader. He also embedded in me the need to put my family first and not travel too much until our boys were grown. He always asked me about Becky and the kids before talking about church or ministry stuff. I am proud to be one of his spiritual sons.
- Jason Chatraw was so helpful in content editing and consulting with me in the process of writing. His friendship during the process was extra special and helped me not give up.
- Thank you Debbie Wichman for doing the first edit to get it moving forward. Your added encouragement was so important. Brooke Turbyfill, thanks for the final editing and getting the book to the end.
- Geoff Olmstead, thanks for your input and designing the cover of *Off Road*. I have always appreciated your creativity and artistry.

- Steve Sjogren who constantly asked me, "When are you going to write that book?" It took awhile but here it is! Thanks Steve.
- For Barbara Chase who opened up her condo in Mexico numerous times, giving me a chance to decompress, reflect and write.
- To Wayne Hendrickson who has been my confidant, counselor, and friend. Thank you for guiding me through some of the hardest times of my life.
- Grateful for the positive examples and influence of leaders God has put in my path along the way. Chuck Smith, John Wimber, Wess Stafford, Luis Bush, Nam Soo Kim, Bob Hoskins, Chad Causey, Hal and Dave Donaldson, Larry Osborne, Rich Nathan, Jackie Pullinger, Menchit Wong, Hap and Diane Leman, Johnny Square, Dary Northrop, David Williams, Ed Davis and Erwin McManus..
- To all the young emerging leaders who have cheered me on in the process. Thank you!
- My Arab friend Afeef Halasah has been especially inspiring to me. Afeef, you are the most humble, fearless and courageous leader I have ever known. Your love and devotion for Arab leaders in the Middle East from Christian and Muslim backgrounds alike is unsurpassed. You continually put your life on the line for those you lead and are under your care. It has been my privilege serving your vision.
- Bruce Clewett (WYAM) has taught me so much and was instrumental in opening doors for me to bring over 400 people on various ministry trips for training, conferences and seminars in Western and Central Europe, particularly among young Catholic Leaders. He was a great coach in teaching me about cross-cultural ministry.

- For the church planters, friends and staff throughout the years at Vineyard Church of the Rockies who have stood by me through thick and thin I salute you. I have learned as much from you as you have from me, maybe more! My life has been made richer by you and you show up on every page here.
- To all who have supported us through the years financially, spiritually and emotionally, Becky and I would not be where we are today without you.

CONTENTS

Preface	xvii
Foreword	xxi
1. Off Road in Vallarta	1
2. Love (Serve) Those You Lead	23
3. Lead from the Inside Out	40
4. Never Be Ashamed of Your Story	58
5. Embrace Your Limp	72
6. Strive to Be a Leader Worth Following	84
7. Just say YES!	98
8. Use it or Lose it: The Futility of Potential	113
9. Refuse Saul's Armor	120
10. Don't Sacrifice Your Life (or Family) on the Altar of Ministry	134
11. Keep Short Accounts	164
12. Lead without Power: Towel vs. the Crown	184
13. Make Sure of Your Calling	198
14. Run "Your" Race	217
Notes	233
About the Author	235

PREFACE
A WORD FROM RICK

IF YOU ARE a young Christian leader who really wants to make an impact in our world and you are willing to go off the beaten path, this book is for you.

There are many books out there that focus on the how-to's of leadership and ministry but not many on how to actually BE a leader. What you are about to read comes from 40 years of hard won lessons and insights some of which have come at great pain and heartache. I want to offer them to you and hope you can avoid some of the pitfalls I have fallen into along the way. Throughout the pages of this book, I will share principles and life lessons from an OG (Old Guard/Original Gangster) in a "no holds barred" approach to leadership and ministry. My goal is to help you as a young leader not only survive but to thrive in ministry.

As I wrote this book, I experienced a wide range of emotions, the kind that come through reflecting on past struggles, failures, and regrets as well as some achievements and breakthroughs. It's a mixed bag for sure, but isn't that true for all of us? However, if my journey and story can benefit you as a young leader just starting out, it is more than worth the effort. The contents of the book came from a question a young leader sprung on me: "What would you say to yourself if you could when you were 23?"

People regularly ask me how long I have worked on writing this book. The short answer is the last eighteen months, but the real answer is over sixty years. My life is a story demonstrating how God can take a nobody from nowhere and use him to do unimaginable things. It's also a story about how God's love triumphs over the negative circumstances of your life. My life is living proof of what is possible if you dare to say yes to God over and over again regardless of your situation.

To Young Leaders

This book is NOT about you, but it is written TO YOU from my heart to yours! You will discover the underbelly of ministry and the realities of what it takes to be a leader who goes the distance. Through my own stories and others, I hope to express various perspectives about what leadership and ministry looks like. You will see the highs and lows that have come from a broken childhood, seven years as a high school teacher, coach and principal, and forty years as a church planter, a senior pastor with a congregation of two thousand, and a pastor to pastors.

A Word to the OGs

I believe we are desperate for this emerging generation to step up and take the lead. For that to happen, they need us OGs alongside them, offering wisdom and encouragement as they face the challenges of their "off road" journey. "Off Road" can also be a useful tool and equipping resource for those of you who desire to serve and mentor this "now" generation of leaders. OGs, young leaders need you and you need them. I get so fired up anytime I get to spend time with them. They remind me that I need to stay in the game, albeit more on the sidelines as a coach instead of a player. OGs, this generation needs spiritual fathers, mothers, grandfathers and grandmothers. Will you be one of them? It just might be part of God's redemptive plan for your life.

Lastly, whether or not you are a pastor in a church or a leader in the marketplace, the principles found here apply to any leader who is passionate about fulfilling the call of God in his or her life. Don't forget that you are a work in progress with God still writing the chapters of your life regardless of what stage you are in.

So buckle up and join me on the "off road" journey of leadership!

Rick Olmstead
March 2023

FOREWORD

WE LIVE IN a world full of 30-second leadership soundbites, clichés, tweets, and Instaposts. Sometimes it feels like the leadership resources we draw from are three miles wide and just one inch deep. Now, I'm not saying those memorable statements aren't valuable—I even have some of them floating around the social media universe. But sometimes we need more substance than just a gummy bear-sized vitamin of leadership inspiration.

That's why God provides us with mentors and role models along the way. People who are along this journey towards influence help us keep our feet grounded, our vision sharp, and decisions life-giving. Imagine what it would be like to be mentored in social justice issues by Martin Luther King, Jr., led into compassion work by Mother Teresa, and taught to preach by T.D. Jakes or Billy Graham, or even taught to inspire learning like that gifted elementary school teacher whose words still impact you today? These are the OG's (Original Gangstas) of leadership and influence. Some we've seen at a distance, known in person, or even caught momentary critical conversations with. Their influence lingers, not just because of what they've said, but by how they've lived. Their fame and credibility didn't propel them to change the world around them; it came because of it.

Here you are as a young leader, pressured by today's Insta-culture to produce fame first and good works as an afterthought. But I suspect something in you longs for authenticity and longevity in your leadership journey. Something in you hopes to find vision not by curation but by inspiration, and through solutions to real-life challenges that have more substance than slacktivism. I have good news.

God's Word is true! Hebrews 12 tells us, "Therefore since we are surrounded by such a great cloud of witnesses, let us throw off everything that hinders and the sin that so easily entangles. And let us run with perseverance the race marked out for us, fixing our eyes on Jesus, the pioneer and perfecter of faith." (NIV) Jesus has your back! And some who have gone before you are ready to cheer for you and coach you along the way. I realize you are inundated by countless and often competing opinions. Learn to listen to voices and wisdom that you know you can trust. Look for leaders with a record of success and willingness to admit their failures.

If your desire is to learn to not only lead well, but also lead long, then this book is for you. Inside these pages you will find the wisdom of a humble OG type of leader. Rick's success isn't just measured by the positions of national and international leadership roles he has held, but the responses I see every time I'm in a room with him sharing with young leaders. Some leaders need to talk loudly to be heard. Other leaders, like Rick Olmstead, only need to whisper and people turn to listen. This book is a compilation of just such wisdom sessions. I know, because I'm a product of his desire to empower and release healthy, equipped, and risk-taking leaders. Leaders who are willing to drive off the predictable roadways of cookie-cutter leadership styles into the land that calls them to higher faith and deeper obedience.

Eric Sandras ("Dr. E")
Author, Lead pastor of Sanctuary Church,
Founder of TheDailySteps.com

ONE
OFF ROAD IN VALLARTA

My wife Becky and I were in Puerto Vallarta, Mexico for a vacation, staying at a nice ocean-front all-inclusive resort. While I was there, I wondered where the people who worked at the resort lived as there were no houses to be seen. One day we rented a motor scooter and went for a ride. As we started driving away from the hotel, I noticed an older woman carrying a bag down a dirt road to seemingly nowhere. Curious where she was headed, I turned down that dirt road after her. What I found was as stunning as the view from our hotel—I stumbled upon a large village composed of native Mexicans. No windows, no paved roads, just lots of people and children all around. I would have never known this existed if I had not ventured off the main road.

That moment really stuck with me. When we only travel on the main road, we only see what is visible around us. There was a whole world right near our hotel, but I couldn't see it until we got off the main road. It's exactly the same as when we stay in the church bubble. We may feel better about ourselves while remaining comfortably inside that bubble, but there is a whole world waiting for what we have to offer. And as you may well know, it's difficult to reach people when we aren't outside our bubble or fortress.

JESUS WAS AN OFF-ROADER

When I reflect on how Jesus conducted his ministry, he sought off-road opportunities at every turn. He did not set up an office where He would wait for people to come to Him. He went to where people were—and took His disciples with Him.

The religious leaders of Jesus' day pressured Him to stay on the main road by following their traditions and ways. Yet time after time He ventured off the main road because there were people who could not be reached from the established religious main road. He went off road when He chose his first disciples, finding a handful of fishermen on the lakeshore. (Who goes to a lake to find your first disciples?) He went off road when he met the woman at Jacob's well. (According to Jewish customs, Jesus wasn't supposed to go there, let alone remain there talking to a woman.) Then there was the woman caught in adultery on the verge of being stoned to death. (Stay out of this, Jesus. You can only lose!) Jesus went way off road when he called a notorious Zacchaeus out of the tree to go have lunch at his house. (What was Jesus thinking?) And then we have Matthew inviting Jesus to a party with all his tax collector guys! (And Jesus went!)

You would think that would be enough, but Jesus thrived off road. He veered off the main to heal the man with the withered hand in the synagogue on the Sabbath, which went against all religious protocol. In various ways, the Pharisees accused Jesus of going off road again and again, such as hanging out with the wrong people and going to the wrong places. "Jesus, you need to stay on the main road with us. This is the way we rabbis and Pharisees do things." But Jesus bucked the religious norms at almost every turn. In response to the Pharisees' warnings, Jesus essentially said, "I can't do that because people are more important to Me than following your man-made traditions."

Today there are a multitude of people who cannot be reached with conventional expressions of church and ministry. It is heartbreaking to see over and over again how expressions of church and ministry are impugned and dismissed by too many in the Christian community. Why would we be so threatened? It's not like what we are doing is working all that well, especially considering that the number of people who identify as Christians has rapidly declined in the West.

It's mind-boggling how contextualizing the gospel in a foreign land to adapt to the local culture is accepted, but such adaptations aren't always embraced when we do it at home. I believe it's critical for the church to continually reinvent itself as we engage a constantly changing culture.

MY OFF-ROAD JOURNEY

After growing up in a very broken family situation in the Los Angeles area, I was taken in by four different families helping me to finish high school, which was no small achievement. These families set my life on a new trajectory.

After high school, I moved back to the L.A. area and enrolled at Cal State, Dominguez Hills, where I played on the golf and baseball teams and encountered Jesus for the first time.

After transferring from Cal State and graduating with a B.A. from Vanguard University, I went to Tehachapi for the summer where my two younger brothers came to live with me. My mom was not really ready to care for children, and that became painfully obvious. They were essentially abandoned by her, and it became my job to be a dad which was quite challenging since I grew up without a dad myself. Looking back on all this, I now realize that God was using all these experiences to shape my leader's heart.

During this time, I started commuting to Cal State University, Bakersfield, which led to a M.A. in education/counseling and a teaching credential that opened the door for me to teach special education and coach in three different high schools in the area. Later on, I launched a Christian coffee house ministry and started a Calvary Chapel Church while still coaching and teaching high school before eventually launching Cummings Valley High School, an alternative high school, and became its first counselor and principal. I was in my sweet spot there, but as good as it was, God had something more. When I reflect on all my life experiences, I realize they prepared me for what was to come.

Meeting John Wimber in 1978 while a part of the Calvary Chapel movement began to change and shape my attitude about pastors and ministry. Prior to that time, I had the idea that God had a "prototype" of what a pastor should be—and I was clearly not one of those. John demonstrated to me that God wasn't looking for cookie cutter leaders or pastors but wanted to use people out of their own personality, gifting, and story.

My first pastors meeting with John was liberating as he showed up in shorts, a Hawaiian shirt, and flip-flops. He talked and acted like a normal person! While I listened to him, he made me think, "Maybe I *can* do this after all." I was drawn to the fact that he was real. He did not use religious jargon or only talk about the victories he experienced but also about his personal struggles. It was the first time I ever heard a prominent leader talk about their struggles, making a major impact on my life since I had struggles of my own. As transparent and humble as Wimber was, he was also a tremendously gifted innovator, risk taker, and leader. God used him to shape my idea of ministry and life as I discovered God simply wanted me to just be me, love Him, and love His people. Yet I still had no idea what being a pastor really entailed.

Life was my first seminary, you might say. I deeply believe God wants to take all of our life's experiences to mold us into what He intends us to be and do. One thing I have learned firsthand is that if you don't curse your life, God can redeem all of it—the good, the bad, and, yes, the ugly.

IS THAT THE PIZZA OR COULD IT BE GOD?

In 1981, my best friend Geoff, whose family took me in to live with them during my eighth and ninth grade years, had recently become engaged and asked me to come and meet his fiancée. My wife Becky and I decided to take a road trip to meet his fiancée in Iowa. Searching for a free place to stay on the way (yes, I was pretty cheap), we ended up routing our trip through Loveland, Colorado to stay with Becky's cousin. The next day we strolled around the neighboring city of Fort Collins before heading off to Cedar Rapids, Iowa.

Upon resuming our trip, we stopped at Shakey's Pizza restaurant in Cheyenne, Wyoming and ate more pizza than anybody should before continuing on I-80 toward Iowa. Somewhere along the way (I'm not sure where exactly because that stretch of land all looked the same to me), I had an overwhelming sensation that I should quit my job and move to Fort Collins to start a church from scratch.

This was a difficult notion to digest as I still did not want to be a pastor and quit the best job of my life which was coaching and being a principal was unthinkable. Such an idea couldn't possibly come from God, right? I wondered if this was the pizza talking or God. (I was hoping it was pizza!) After wrestling with this idea for a while as I drove, I decided I needed to run this by Becky, who was a school teacher and also loved what she was doing. If this was God, then we would both have to give up our jobs, which wouldn't be an easy decision.

I asked Becky if she felt like God was saying anything to her about that town we'd strolled through the day before. She innocently said no and wanted to know why I was asking. I swallowed hard and told her what I was feeling and she emphatically said, "Well, God is not saying anything to me." We decided from that point on that we would not move forward in this unless we both were in agreement. During the next few weeks, we explored the possibilities while looking for confirmation—and it came in various ways. We were both still secretly hoping that this was the pizza I ate and not God so I could go back into the education field where I had earned a Master of Arts degree in education/counseling and put this pastor thing to rest.

But the further we explored the idea, the more convinced we became that this was the next step God wanted us to take in our lives. So once we finished our contract with the school district, we loaded our U-haul (and our dog Ike) and headed to Colorado in the summer of 1982 with little money, no place to live, and more questions than answers about this crazy adventure. Our first night there, we slept on the floor of a friend's house and had our first meeting the next day with seven people.

FEAR OF REGRET OVER FEAR OF FAILURE

A Wheaton college football coach was riding a bike in a triathlon when he saw the back of the shirt ahead with a phrase that stunned him: *Don't die wondering*. Subsequently, he incorporated that as his team's motto. You can forever wonder about the what-ifs of your life, or you can seize the moments as they present themselves and not look back.

At one point in the process, the bigger risk for me and Becky wasn't going to Colorado and failing, but instead it was not obeying this call and wondering for the rest of our lives if this was what God had in store for us. The fear of regret became greater than our fear of failure. We thought the worst case was we would have to start over with substitute teaching and eventually get teaching jobs again, so we had to try it and see if this was God after all. The certainty of this call sustained us many times when we were tempted to give up and quit. (Most Mondays, right?) The words kept coming from the Lord: "Have I not called you here? This is not about you and what you can do but what I can and will do." This is why having a sense of calling is so important in what we do.

Years later, "Was it pizza or was it God?" became folklore in our church. The answer now seems evident as the church grew from those seven initial people into thousands of participants and 30-plus pastors being sent out to start new churches or take over existing ones. Never in a million years would I have guessed what

God was going to do through two clueless people who knew little about pastoring and ministry in general.

ME? A PASTOR? SAY IT ISN'T SO!

When it came to my experience in the church, I was a neophyte for sure after having been raised outside the church by a single mom. I had a life-changing encounter with Jesus my first year of college that would change the trajectory of my life, but the idea of church and all that went with it was still quite foreign to me. It was a subculture that I had to learn. I did not get the dress, the haircuts, the songs, the sermons—nothing made sense nor did anyone try to help it make sense to me. The few times I did visit a church growing up, it felt very empty, non-compelling, and quite irrelevant to my life. I did not find Jesus in those instances nor was I ever invited to.

Becky, on the other hand, came from a very stable Christian family who went to church all her life and understood the ins and outs of church life. (I learned the hard way never to play Bible trivia with anyone in her family.) This shaped our approach to church. Becky had a huge heart for those inside the church, and I had a big heart for those outside looking in. Apparently God knew what he was doing after all when He put me and Becky together to start our church. Going off road in terms of how we did ministry became the norm for the next season of our lives.

WHO LET *THEM* IN?

I can relate to the outcome of the Jerusalem Council in Acts 15 where they dealt with the issue of Gentiles who didn't know all the Jewish customs. Paul and Peter, who were trying to help church leaders navigate this issue, had plenty of experience in venturing off the main road to fulfill the call of God in their lives. Then James joined them as he made a huge "off road" stand to suggest the Gentiles did not have to follow all the Jewish customs, which would be a tremendous obstacle in their new journey of faith.

In Acts 15:10-11, Peter challenges the council: "Now then, why do you try to test God by putting on the necks of Gentiles a yoke that neither we nor our ancestors have been able to bear? No! We believe it is through the grace of our Lord Jesus that we are saved, just as they are." (New International Version) Then in verse 19, James chimes in: **"It is my judgment, therefore, that we should not make it difficult for the Gentiles who are turning to God."** (Acts 15:19 NIV)

We should do everything we possibly can to make it easy for people to come to Jesus. At that point, there is a decision to make: yes to following Jesus or walk away. The cost of following Jesus is not negotiable—it never was and can't be today. But I find that many believers have memory lapse as they forget what it's like being on the outside looking in.

Yet, you might object, "Wait a minute. Didn't Jesus say that He was the narrow way and few enter in?" You would be correct, but the Western church tends to make it narrower with all of our add-ons, which become unnecessary barriers. Sometimes these additional requirements and expectations make it nearly impossible for people to come to Jesus in the way we demand. Sadly, it's similar to what Jesus faced with the Pharisees. Now, these aren't major doctrinal shifts but might include liturgy, music style, dress, pet doctrines, or our particular Christian subculture. Sometimes we don't realize just how weird we look to those on the outside. Instead of being peculiar in a bad way, we need to make the good news of Jesus understandable and accessible to as many as possible, much in the same way that God designed the Temple to include a place—the Court of the Gentile—for seekers to come to begin their journey of faith.

Young leaders, you do not have to apologize for making room for outsiders. In fact, Jesus constantly drew the ire of religious leaders as He became renowned (and accused) of being a "friend of sinners" and loving people in the margins. Not a bad thing to be known for if you ask me. Jesus met people where they were and offered Himself to them. Our main job is to get people to Jesus. A good question to ask ourselves: Are we building bridges to Jesus or erecting barriers that keep people away? I agree with Jesus' brother James in Acts 15 when he urged the Jerusalem Council to make it as easy as possible for people to come to Christ.

CULTURE SHOCK

When I look at the church, I see a group of people whose job is supposed to be about building bridges, not barriers, to those who are coming to Christ. The only barrier is Jesus Christ Himself, not the road to Him. I hope you will find and build new bridges for people to find Jesus who live in the off-road culture around us today.

Whether we admit it or not, we have to face the fact that some of our most cherished expressions may be our own brand of cultural Christianity here in America. Have you noticed that what worked fifty, forty, thirty or even twenty years ago isn't as effective today if it even works at all? Insanity, according to Albert Einstein, is "doing the same thing over and over again expecting a different result."

Our first step may need to be admitting that what we are doing is *not* working any more. Our biggest obstacle may be our past successes. And if we're going to forge effective ministry pathways, we shouldn't tear down new attempts to explore ministry and church outside the traditional box; rather, we should celebrate their efforts, stand with them, and root them on.

I believe if we are going to reach a generation with the good news of Jesus, it will take a new breed of courageous leaders—perhaps someone like you—who are willing to go off road and discover new and fresh expressions of doing ministry and church. Like Jesus, you might feel similar pressure to stay on the main road and fall in line with those who have gone before you. But what about all those people you can't see, reach, or get to from the traditional religious main road? Maybe it's time to take a dirt road detour and see where it leads *without* judging those who remain on the main traditional road.

HONOR THOSE WHO'VE GONE BEFORE

Contrary to popular opinion, your life is not ruled by either/or choices. You can (and should)—at the same time—honor and bless long-cherished traditions and expressions of the church while going boldly on your off-road adventure. As you go, make the effort to bless and ask for blessings from those who have gone before you. Yes, some may be less than excited about your off-road journey, misjudge you, and even challenge you, but bless and forgive them regardless. Jesus Himself cried, "Father, forgive them for they do not know what they are doing." (Luke 23:34 NIV)

Off-road leadership requires courage as you go against the current of prevalent thinking. It's about taking risks, exploring uncharted territories, and leading others through uncertain terrain. I believe that many of you "now generation" leaders need to go off road and connect not only with new people but discover new wineskins and models of ministry. It's not like my generation figured out the magic blueprint for church ministry to be used for infinity.

Yet it's not about going rogue or being rebellious; it's about pushing (or knocking down) unnecessary barriers that have kept people from coming to Jesus, and have kept the church confined to obscurity and irrelevancy. You can be an advocate and champion for those who are unchurched or far away from God.

At the same time, this is not about being a "deconstructionist" either, blowing up everything. Instead, it's about building on the foundations already established. Young leaders, if you don't bless the past and those who have been a part of your journey, you unintentionally put obstacles in your path and in the paths of those you lead. The way forward is always blessing the way you came.

Don't feel like you are doing something wrong because you are not following exactly in our footsteps. I think it may be our insecurity that restrains us from blessing you, but give us time and we will come around.

What I hear from many younger generation leaders is that although you may not choose to follow in our footsteps, you still value and need us older leaders. You are not dishonoring us if you don't want to sing our songs, follow our music style, or listen to our sermons (some are really good), or even do church a certain way.

Recently, as I was re-watching the movie *The Intern* with some friends, the younger people in our group referred to Robert De Niro as "vintage." Like fine wine, better with age? I like that—"vintage leaders." I guess I am now one of them! If wine gets better with age, why can't we? So Vintage OG (Original Gangsters, Old Guard or Old Guys?), it doesn't matter what you call us, but you need us and we need you. I often hear young leaders say that you don't want us to tell you what or how to do everything, but I believe you desire our counsel when you ask. Sometimes we OG's need to be asked or we are not sure how or when we can contribute. So please press in when you need us.

DON'T GO ALONE!

Going off road is not meant to be a solo journey. Jesus did not send His disciples out one by one but two by two and sometimes even more. Paul, Peter, and others went out as a team as they explored new horizons of ministry. Leonard Sweet once said, "Today you can find anything you want on the internet, but you can't find wisdom and experience."

Before you go, strengthen those who are older and then take some of us OGs with you. And remember that we who are older are not done yet either. Yes, it's true. We, like Caleb of old, still have some gas in the tank. Our wisdom and counsel may be helpful to you along the way. And you need spiritual moms and dads alongside you too, not just for you but for those you reach. If God is turning the hearts of the children back to their parents and vice-versa, you're going to want spiritual fathers and mothers (grandfathers and mothers too).

A great picture of this is Moses and young Joshua. Moses let Joshua choose his young warriors and sent them out to fight the Amalekites. While they were out fighting the battle, others were holding up Moses' arms, and together the victory was secured. Quite the teamwork of the young and old working together.

As Joshua grew older, he listened, honored, and faithfully served Moses, not realizing that one day it would be his turn to lead Israel through a huge turning point in the nation's history. What a sight as Moses watched from Mount Nebo (present day Jordan) as Joshua led the children off road into the land of promise. Moses was sad that he couldn't go but so proud of his spiritual son, Joshua, as he rooted him on.

I can't emphasize enough your need to know the *why* and not just the *what* of what you plan to do as you go. Your best ideas won't take you very far but will end in frustration. You need to believe you are doing what God has called you to do. The reason to go off road is because God has put something in your heart and mind that cannot be achieved by staying on the main road. Don't go because you are unhappy, frustrated, and impatient but because God *and* your leaders affirm it's time to go!

BATON VERSUS THE TORCH

I used to coach high school track and, like most, I really loved the relay events. It's one of the rare teamwork moments during a track meet with the passing of the baton requiring extreme precision and concentration. If you pass the baton too early or too late, it can mean disqualification, discounting all the effort everyone put into the race.

There's one more piece of the relay that's a great picture of transition. During the handoff, there is a brief period of time when both runners are running at full speed together. Each runner goes all out until that last gasp and then hands the baton to the next runner. After you hand it off, you are supposed to have nothing left as the next runner takes off.

In discussing ministry transitions, we often use the analogy of passing the baton to the next generation of leaders. However, it has some challenges. The issue I have with it in our ministry and leadership context is that those of us who are older tend to hold on to that baton much too long. Why is that? Because we know something. We know that when we hand that ministry baton off, we are done, so we hold on to it as long as we can. Then, when we finally decide to hand it off to the younger generation, oftentimes there is no one to hand it to because the younger generation had to go somewhere else to be who God called you to be. And for those who do stick around, I hear you saying, "What makes you think we want to inherit what you created anyway?" *Ouch!* I used to think, "Of course you want to continue with what I have started (staying on the main road) when it's your time." How wrong I was!

TORCH BEARERS ALL

Here's another idea. What if we create a future together where we who are older are not put out to pasture or on the shelf but stay in the game alongside you? What if instead of the baton, we think in terms of being torch bearers? We light each other's fire over and over again. When yours goes out, I am there to light yours, and when mine goes dim, you can re-light mine. Nobody becomes irrelevant, set aside, and unvalued. What if we become those intergenerational people who stand together, turning the tide and making a real difference in our world? So many churches today are either young people churches or old people churches but what if churches today had a mixture of young and older leaders working hand in hand together? Could we see a revival of epic proportions? I think it's possible! What do we have to lose?

My friend Hap Leman helped me understand this idea by something his dad said to him over and over again. "As a young man farming with horses you put two horse teams together. The ideal horse team had an older wise horse and a younger strong horse. The old one knew what to do and where to go, and the younger horse had the strength and stamina to pull the weight." Hap never forgot this, and it has shaped his attitude of embracing an intergenerational vision.

OG's, when you finish one race, another one is about to begin if you dare to embrace it. Don't believe the lie that you are done! You may not be able to do what you used to do, but there is still more in the tank for the tasks God has in store for you. One of the reasons I stepped down from leading our church after 37 years is that I came to a place where I realized I did not have the energy or stamina to be what our church needed. The church needed more than I was able to give. It was hard to admit, but letting go was not only the best for the church but also for me. Closing one door opened up a new door that is allowing me to pursue my passion of fathering a new generation of young leaders. This book is an expression of that new assignment and would not have happened if I had not let go of what I had. I have never been more excited than I am right now for what God has given me to do. OG's, you don't have to hold on fearing that if you do, it's over for you. It just might be the beginning of something new!!

Maybe all this is part of going off road and blazing some new trails. Who knows what might happen? I am a vintage OG leader who is not done going off road either, and writing this book is part of that journey too. So my encouragement to you, young leaders, is to consider—or reconsider—those wild, out-of-the-box ideas that don't go away. It just might be God speaking to you, but you will never know unless you take a step in that direction and say *yes* to what seems impossible. We need new models and new wineskins if we are to effectively engage the culture we live in. I believe you can find them. They may even already be in you!

There has never been a more challenging time to be a leader or pastor than today. It can also be the most exciting time as we enter a moment where we can bring living hope to a world reaching a deep point of despair. Our world is losing hope more by the day. Yet hope lives because Jesus lives, and we are carriers of that hope. Desperate times require desperate measures. Yes, leading in our churches today has many unique issues, and I believe you are up for that challenge!

A Church for the Crazy Ones?
by Eric Sandras

The Sanctuary Story: "Son, you have spent your entire life letting your circumstances influence your belief in me. When things are going well, you believe I'm happy with you. When things are rough, you think I'm mad at you. This season of your life, I'm going to teach you to let your belief in Me influence your circumstances. Just do what I've called you to do and care for those in the margins. My grace is always sufficient for you." That's not the answer I expected from God as I was in the midst of telling him I didn't want to be GIVEN a building as a brand new church start!

Trust me, I had good reasons why I didn't want to be given a sixty-thousand-square-foot, debt-free, former Baptist campus with a complete kitchen and gymnasium and an auditorium that could seat just north of two hundred people.

First, I reminded the Lord I wasn't looking for a building. I was just looking to rent a room on Wednesday nights for a recovery meeting!

Second, I told the Lord that I refuse to become building- and Sunday-performance-centric again in my leadership and life. I've served in too many churches where all they could think, meet, and talk about was the next Sunday gig.

And finally, my clincher was, "God, you just got the wrong

guy. I just want a little church that cares for the poor and the margins—find a manager not an entrepreneur."

Of course God's answer sank deep into my soul, because I've learned to allow His voice to carry more weight than my emotions or logic. *"Just do what I've asked you to do and care for the margins..."* Those words have carried me through nine years of miracles and challenges.

What if, as leaders, we prayed for our city and community, not just our church? How would our behaviors and priorities change? The Sanctuary Church has committed to being a church that strives to spend 80% of its time, energy, and resources on 80% of our community's needs, not on church needs. The Sanctuary Church moved into that facility just a few months after the offer. Before I could even figure out where all the light switches were, the miracles started happening. Today, our little group of ragamuffins leads recovery meetings almost seven days per week, runs a food pantry that distributes over ten-thousand pounds of food per month, hosts a counseling center for under-resourced individuals and families, provides a café that serves two-hundred free breakfasts to the homeless every Sunday morning, and has developed a prison correspondence program currently in six prisons in three different states.

As a young leader, be sure your vision and calling is from the Holy Spirit Himself. I often ask disillusioned leaders, "Who were you called to be before other leaders started to tell you who you ought to be?" Remember, you walk in a reality far greater than the business management culture you are taught to live in. The Kingdom of God plays by its own rules. Use the experience of OG leaders, the wisdom of The Holy Spirit Himself, and your tenacity and passion to pursue your calling. It'll come together! Finally, keep in mind that success in the Kingdom is not necessarily about outcome, but it is always about obedience.

—Eric Sandras, Lead pastor of The Sanctuary Church
TSCwest.org and TheDailySteps.com
Author of Buck Naked Faith *and* When the Sky is Falling

GENERATION NOW

THIS IS YOUR TIME, your opportunity! You are the *Now* Generation, not just the *Next* Generation. I believe that next-gen language is not all that helpful as it can send the wrong message. Too often that message is that your day is always tomorrow or someday but never today. So, what do you need right now to be who God has called you to be? That is what we OG's want and need to give you. Typically, we invested in the next generation and hoped it somehow works when the time comes. There is no sense of urgency in that because the "next" is way out there in the "land of someday."

You may be more ready than you think or have been told. God has a history of using people who thought they were not ready. I pray that God will awaken the dream He has for your life and the world in which we live. God wants to give you your own stories and your own experiences as His Kingdom is being released in and through you. So like God told Gideon in Judges 6:14 (NIV), *"...Go in the strength that you have, and save Israel out of Midian's hand. Am I not sending you?"* And to Joshua, *"...Be strong and courageous. Do not be afraid; do not be discouraged, for the Lord your God will be with you wherever you go"* (Joshua 1:9 NIV). That was not a someday challenge but a right-now call on his life. Like many of us, Gideon did not think he was ready for such a huge task, but God obviously didn't agree. So, young leader, bring what you have to the table and say *yes* to the steps God opens up to you. A new Jesus revolution needs and requires leaders like you and it's a 'now' proposition. The church and the world needs leaders like you who are passionately in love with Jesus and His Kingdom and willing to lay down their life for others. Your time is today, not tomorrow, and you are Generation Now!

"HERE'S TO THE CRAZY ONES"

"Here's to the crazy ones. The misfits. The rebels. The troublemakers. The round pegs in the square holes. The ones who see things differently. They're not fond of rules. And they have no respect for the status quo. You can quote them, disagree with them, glorify or vilify them. About the only thing you can't do is ignore them. Because they change things. They push the human race forward. And while some may see them as the crazy ones, we see genius. Because the people who are crazy enough to think they can change the world, are the ones who do."

— Written by John Chapman (1774-1845) and popularized by Rob Siltanen and Steve Jobs

So, my young friend, fly like the eagles and say yes to His yes in your life, and prepare to let the off-road adventure begin. You have a voice and your voice needs to be heard. There might be more of us than you think who are ready to listen! A new *Jesus Revolution* is coming, and you are going to lead it!

QUESTIONS FOR THE HEART

1. What does going off road look like for you?

2. Why is it important to go with blessing?

3. What outside-the-box thoughts do you have when you think about ministry and church?

4. How have you dealt with disillusionment in your life, ministry or relationships? Describe.

5. Do you agree with the idea of an intergenerational ministry? As a young leader, what do you believe needs to change for that to happen? Explain.

6. If you are Generation Now, what are the implications of that? What does that change?

WHEN I WAS 23 …

The following chapters began from an unexpected question I had from Jared, a young leader I met who had an obvious call on his life. One day after we'd met for a few hours, he said he had one more question for me. I invited his question, unaware of what was coming. "What would you say to yourself if you could when you were 23?" he asked. I was both stunned and surprised by it, especially by the fact that immediately something came to mind.

I grew up in Gardena and South Los Angeles—in a very broken home where I was staying up all night and barely going to school. My eighth grade year, I went to live with my best friend's family through ninth grade. Then on to the small town of Tehachapi where three different families took me in and helped get me through high school. After a life-changing encounter with Jesus in my second year of college and later graduating from Vanguard University, I wanted to give back to that special community who had taken me in and provided me with so many opportunities. So I went back to Tehachapi, now as a follower of Jesus to do ministry for the summer before going to grad school.

Toward the end of that summer, I got a call from my mother that she could not handle my 15-year-old brother and wanted me to take him. I knew saying *yes* to my mom would mean saying no to grad school that fall.

But I said *yes,* and my brother Mike came to live with me and we had some great times together. A month later, I got a second call to take my other brother Mark, who was 13 years old. Again I said *yes*. Fortunately, over the next five years, they were able to graduate from high school and excel in various sports. At the same time, since I was only 23, it was quite the challenge caring and providing for two teenage boys while working multiple jobs. I tried to be the big brother and a father figure too—which I had no idea how to be since I grew up without a father myself. Interesting note—before I became a Christian and when I was still in high school, I kind of prayed (wished) for my brothers to get the same chance at a new life as I did. Who would have guessed that years later I would be the answer to that wish (prayer)?

When Jared asked that question, I immediately knew the first thing I would say to myself: "Rick, your brothers are more important than your ministry. Give your best to them and make them your top priority." I did NOT do this and, sadly, I let working, ministry, teaching, and coaching get the best of my time. As a result, my brothers lost out and so did I. Please don't let ministry, work, or anything else rob you and others of what matters most! I have tried to give myself some grace in all this as I did not have a dad and had an overwhelming situation thrust upon me. Yes, I did the best I could with what I had, but my best was not always good for them.

So here we go; may these lessons, stories and insights inspire and encourage you on your off-road journey.

TWO
LOVE (SERVE) THOSE YOU LEAD

LOVE PEOPLE like God has loved you. Your number one job description as a leader is to love the people you serve. People really can tell if you love them or not. They know if you are going through the motions. I had a woman come up to me after a service when I ended by saying, "I love being your pastor" (which was true). She said that meant so much for her to hear me say that I loved being her pastor. I was surprised but never forgot that and realized that the people I lead need to know and hear that I love them. Just like in marriage, we need to show AND tell our spouse over and over again how much we love them. Our church—yours and mine—needs that from us as well. A board member of a church (not mine) once told me that she does not think her pastor likes the people of her church. And sadly in that case, knowing her pastor, I think she might be right.

1 Peter 5:1-4 (NLT) puts it like this:

> *And now, a word to you who are elders in the churches. I, too, am an elder and a witness to the sufferings of Christ. And I, too, will share in* his *glory when* he *is revealed to the whole world. As a fellow elder, I appeal to you: Care for the flock that God has entrusted to you. Watch over it willingly, not grudgingly—not for*

what you will get out of it, but because you are eager to serve God. Don't lord it over the people assigned to your care, but lead them by your own good example. And when the Great Shepherd appears, you will receive a crown of never-ending glory and honor.

Peter follows up by reminding us that we are to shepherd God's people not because we have to but because we want to. Jesus laid down His life for us, His sheep, because He loved us. His love for His father and for people drove Him to the cross and kept Him there until he finished what he came to do. "For the joy set before him he endured the cross" (Hebrews 12:2 NIV). Remember? That joy was you and me.

The great commandment is for leaders too: "... 'Love the Lord your God with all your heart and with all your soul and with all your strength and with all your mind'; and, 'Love your neighbor as yourself'" (Luke 10:27 NIV).

If your people do not feel loved by you, your preaching becomes like white noise. Too many leaders are angry at their people because they don't do what they want them to do, or give what they want them to give or share their faith like they want them to. You likely understand this all too well. Unfortunately, that frustration bleeds all over the church. We end up becoming a cattle driver as we push people like cattle where we want them to be rather than lead by example as they follow us.

You can have great strategies, big vision, and powerful sermons, but if you don't have love, you're like "a noisy gong or a clanging cymbal" (1 Cor. 13:1 NLT). Lead with love and let love win the day! Sometimes I think it's a lot easier to love people "out there" than the ones right here who have names and faces you know. Yes, for sure love the "lost," but don't forget about the Jose's, David's, Rachel's, and Chandra's who are right in front of you. The Bible says there are many teachers but not many fathers. The church today is desperate for spiritual moms and dads. Find one or be one!

EVERYONE HATES EVANGELISM, RIGHT?

My friend Steve Sjogren said in his powerful book, *The Conspiracy of Kindness*, "The one thing Christians and non-Christians have in common is that they both hate Evangelism." Why is that? People hate being at the end of someone's projects, even good ones. People are perceptive and can tell if you really care about them or if you're doing a feel-better-about-yourself project and trying to add another notch on your Bible. I admit too many times, I gave a monologue rather than listening to people, showing very little interest in getting to know the person. I believe that stranger evangelism is strange evangelism—and quite foreign to the way we see Jesus operating in the Bible. Learning to listen and finding out what's going on in people's lives takes time and effort. But that's what love does—it travels and takes the time to love. Lead with love and watch what happens.

As a new believer, I was up for almost anything if it would help people enter into a relationship with Jesus. I once found a group of Christians who were going door to door "doing evangelism." Afterward they would go on the radio and share incredible results. So, I went with them one Friday night and gave it a go despite not being excited about the door-to-door thing. What I realized was that the only goal was to get them to "pray the prayer" with little regard for what was happening in their life. There was little interest in hearing their story because we had another door to knock on. We had a plan and stuck to it regardless of the condition of the person we were talking to, and it began to grieve my heart.

One particular night, we met with a single mom who was obviously in great distress and struggling with life and especially with her kids. The leader of our group completely ignored her situation but got her to say the prayer. (Ever notice that Jesus never tried to get people to "pray the prayer"?) There was no offer to acknowledge her need, help her, or even pray for her situation. Then we went back to the radio station where the leader shared the wonderful story of this woman giving her life to Christ. I actually felt sick to my stomach, unsure if the only reason she prayed "the prayer" was to get rid of us. Even though I was a brand new believer myself, I knew that this was not for me and never went back. That's not to malign the effort or hearts of those who engage in this type of evangelism. But I wonder if we somehow cheapen the gospel by telling people to "just pray these magic words and heaven is yours." The work of real discipleship requires blood, sweat, and tears, not a persuasive argument and a repeatable prayer.

Reaching lost people is clearly *part* of our mission—but how we do it really matters. Too often the end has come to justify the means. Jesus engaged people where they were at, like the woman at Jacob's well, Zacchaeus in a tree, Matthew at his tax collector booth, and many others. (John 4:1-26; Luke 19:1-10; Matthew 9:9-13) Going off road is realizing that the Great Commission in Matthew 28:16-20 is more about our *going* than about their *coming*. Our mandate from Jesus is to seek and to save those who are lost. That means organizing search parties and going to where they are! If you want to reach the lost of our world, you need to meet them on their turf. Yes, it might get dicey and you might find yourself in uncomfortable situations, but over time you will realize they are just people like you in search of something more.

THE SHAPING OF A LEADER'S HEART

While serving at our most recent church in California's central coast, our property was on sixty-five acres, and every year, there were local shepherds who brought their sheep and goats to graze. I was amazed at all the work and planning that went into what they did before the sheep/goats even arrived. They put up a temporary fence to keep the sheep corralled before moving the fence to another area after they had eaten all the grass. I was captured by how the shepherds watched over the sheep and knew what they needed and when they needed to move to greener pastures. These shepherds led the sheep into the pens, while cattle drivers in the area would direct their herd with a whip. The results may be the same, but the methods are quite different. The life of a shepherd is challenging, yet because of their love for their sheep, the animals are safe and grow up strong and healthy. If you've been in ministry long, I'm sure you can relate.

CATTLE DRIVERS OR SHEPHERDS

I believe that God's leaders are to be focused more on people than on strategies and programs. Or put more succinctly, "People are more important than programs." I love strategy as much as anyone, but people can get left behind and lost in the shuffle of our strategies. We are to be shepherds, not cattle drivers. We are called to love, lead and feed God's sheep (people). There it is in a nutshell! We aren't called to be cattle drivers, whipping people into submission. Sadly that's how some old-school churches operated, forcing the congregation to sit through sermons that beat you up for how awful you are and how God (or the pastor) is not pleased with you. I was in on some of that nonsense in my earlier days. Some Sundays ended up being a "beat-the sheep-Sunday" by a very frustrated pastor—and I hated it.

We need to *go* the way, not just point the way. Sheep follow their shepherds while they run from the drivers. Pastors and Christian leaders should smell like sheep! Sadly, too many don't. I've talked to a number of pastors who admit they don't really like people that much (their words, not mine) or being around them. Why would you want to be a pastor if you are not into people? I don't get it! We are not CEOs, presidents, or professionals; we are God's leaders and shepherds. But sadly, too many pastors are locked up in their studies and have little connection with the people they talk to on Sundays, wholly unaware of what people are going through in their day-to-day lives. Some are completely out of touch with what's happening in the real world. Jesus was called Immanuel—God with the people—and we should be "leaders and shepherds with the people."

It was during these years taking care of my brothers and figuring out who I was, that God began to shape my leader heart. David was called a "man after God's own heart," and that is what qualified him to be the leader he was meant to be. (1 Samuel 13:14 NIV) Without the heart, nothing else really matters. Spiritual leadership is first and foremost a matter of the heart. When leaders lose heart, everyone loses. The Bible mentions the heart 715 times. The great commandment begins with "love the Lord your God with all your heart" (Luke 10:27 NIV). In Luke 6:45, Jesus tells us, "A good man brings good things out of the good stored up in his heart." (NIV). Solomon tells us in Proverbs 4:23, "Above all else, guard your heart, for everything you do flows from it" (NIV). Leadership at the end of the day boils down to what is in the heart. If you break the heart of a leader, you break the leader!

A PICTURE OF CHURCH FROM UGANDA

I recently returned from a trip to Uganda and the Watoto Church, one of the most authentic pictures of what a church can be—with over 35,000 members, including 30,000 in small groups. But what's most incredible is how they serve the poor and broken of their city. They have created what they call Watoto villages in the midst of extremely impoverished areas where they rescue orphans and abandoned children, including babies left in the local dump, streets and hospital door steps. The church takes these abandoned babies and kids and gives them a home. This congregation has built four hundred homes that each house four boys, four girls and a house mom. I was so overwhelmed with emotion as I witnessed what a church pursuing the heart of Jesus is capable of looking like. They have a church, a school, a medical clinic, and vocational opportunities as they give kids a chance at a life they could not even imagine.

During my trip there, I had the privilege to share my story with two of the Watoto village churches. The pastors and leaders of Watoto are very incarnational. They live and serve among those they lead. Every pastor we met had a huge heart of compassion for their people as many came from great personal struggles and heartache themselves. The smell of sheep was everywhere, and it was so refreshing!

In my early days as a pastor, I realized the importance of staying connected to our community. But leading a church requires plenty of energy and it's not always easy to do. So, I took on a position with the Fort Collins Police Department as a chaplain that lasted 20 years to stay grounded in my community. What kind of opportunities can you see to connect with your community?

While there are some bad apples that seem to get most of the press, there are also some amazing servant leaders who have a deep love for God and His kingdom. Many pastors start off well but lose their way along the journey. Many became bitter, jaded, and angry at God—and the people they are supposed to serve. You probably know some pastors who have fallen prey to this.

But understand this: You are God's gift to your church AND the community you live in.

Jeremiah 3:15 says: "Then I will give you shepherds after my own heart, who will lead you with knowledge and understanding" (NIV).

We are God's gift to our churches, shepherds after his own heart to lead and serve his people. I believe this is what God is doing today. Bringing forth a new breed of servant leaders who lay down their lives for those they serve (and not the other way around.) I believe most pastors have a big heart for God and His people and are doing the best they can and need our support.

Perspective and perception are vital to helping you walk out this type of pastoring. When you think of people you lead or will lead, do you see them existing for you, or do you see yourself being there for them? Too many pastors get frustrated with the people they lead because they are in the way of them succeeding in their ministry. You exist first for God and secondly to love and serve His people. They are His people, not your people. He alone is the great shepherd over His flock of which we are a part. As His under-shepherds, we are stewards, not owners, and we will give an account one day on how we did caring for and leading His people.

In John 10:11-13, Jesus declares, "I am the good shepherd. The good shepherd lays down his life for the sheep" (NIV). The hired hand is not a true shepherd and does not own the sheep. So when he or she sees the wolf coming, they abandon the sheep and run away. Then the wolf attacks the flock, devouring and scattering it. He runs away because he is a hired hand and cares only for himself, not for the sheep.

True shepherds do not abandon the sheep in hard and dangerous times. The captain lays down his life for the ship just like the shepherd lays down his life for the church! This is how it was meant to be. Christians need more examples that portray the type of leadership that Jesus desires from His leaders today. People will not be more committed, selfless, and courageous than those who lead them! Unfortunately, we have not always given young leaders a great picture of what this looks like. This might be why some of our best leaders look elsewhere than the church to make a difference. That narrative needs to change.

YOU CAN'T LEAD PEOPLE WELL IF YOU DON'T LOVE THEM

Love people like God has loved you. Your number one job description as a leader is to love the people you serve. People really can tell if you love them or not. They know if you are going through the motions. I had a woman come up to me after a service when I ended by saying, "I love being your pastor" (which was true). She said that meant so much for her to hear me say that I loved being her pastor. I was surprised but never forgot that and realized that the people I lead need to know and hear that I love them. Just like in marriage, we need to show AND tell our spouse over and over again how much we love them. Our church—yours and mine—needs that from us as well. A board member of a church (not mine) once told me that she does not think her pastor likes the people of her church. And sadly in that case, knowing her pastor, I think she might be right.

1 Peter 5:1-4 (NLT) puts it like this:

> *And now, a word to you who are elders in the churches. I, too, am an elder and a witness to the sufferings of Christ. And I, too, will share in his glory when he is revealed to the whole world. As a fellow elder, I appeal to you: Care for the flock that God has entrusted to you. Watch over it willingly, not grudgingly—not for what you will get out of it, but because you are eager to serve God. Don't lord it over the people assigned to your care, but lead them by your own good example. And when the Great Shepherd appears, you will receive a crown of never-ending glory and honor.*

Peter follows up by reminding us that we are to shepherd God's people not because we have to but because we want to. Jesus laid down His life for us, His sheep, because He loved us. His love for His father and for people drove Him to the cross and kept Him there until he finished what he came to do. "For the joy set before him he endured the cross" (Hebrews 12:2 NIV). Remember? That joy was you and me.

The great commandment is for leaders too: "... 'Love the Lord your God with all your heart and with all your soul and with all your strength and with all your mind'; and, 'Love your neighbor as yourself'" (Luke 10:27 NIV).

If your people do not feel loved by you, your preaching becomes like white noise. Too many leaders are angry at their people because they don't do what they want them to do, or give what they want them to give or share their faith like they want them to. You likely understand this all too well. Unfortunately, that frustration bleeds all over the church. We end up becoming a cattle driver as we push people like cattle where we want them to be rather than lead by example as they follow us.

You can have great strategies, big vision, and powerful sermons, but if you don't have love, you're like "a noisy gong or a clanging cymbal" (1 Cor. 13:1 NLT). Lead with love and let love win the day! Sometimes I think it's a lot easier to love people "out there" than the ones right here who have names and faces you know. Yes, for sure love the "lost," but don't forget about the Jose's, David's, Rachel's, and Chandra's who are right in front of you. The Bible says there are many teachers but not many fathers. The church today is desperate for spiritual moms and dads. Find one or be one!

EVERYONE HATES EVANGELISM, RIGHT?

My friend Steve Sjogren said in his powerful book, *The Conspiracy of Kindness*, "The one thing Christians and non-Christians have in common is that they both hate Evangelism." Why is that? People hate being at the end of someone's projects, even good ones. People are perceptive and can tell if you really care about them or if you're doing a feel-better-about-yourself project and trying to add another notch on your Bible. I admit too many times, I gave a monologue rather than listening to people, showing very little interest in getting to know the person. I believe that stranger evangelism is strange evangelism—and quite foreign to the way we see Jesus operating in the Bible. Learning to listen and finding out what's going on in people's lives takes time and effort. But that's what love does—it travels and takes the time to love. Lead with love and watch what happens.

As a new believer, I was up for almost anything if it would help people enter into a relationship with Jesus. I once found a group of Christians who were going door to door "doing evangelism." Afterward they would go on the radio and share incredible results. So, I went with them one Friday night and gave it a go despite not being excited about the door-to-door thing. What I realized was that the only goal was to get them to "pray the prayer" with little regard for what was happening in their life. There was little interest in hearing their story because we had another door to knock on. We had a plan and stuck to it regardless of the condition of the person we were talking to, and it began to grieve my heart.

One particular night, we met with a single mom who was obviously in great distress and struggling with life and especially with her kids. The leader of our group completely ignored her situation but got her to say the prayer. (Ever notice that Jesus never tried to get people to "pray the prayer"?) There was no offer to acknowledge her need, help her, or even pray for her situation. Then we went back to the radio station where the leader shared the wonderful story of this woman giving her life to Christ. I actually felt sick to my stomach, unsure if the only reason she prayed "the prayer" was to get rid of us. Even though I was a brand new believer myself, I knew that this was not for me and never went back. That's not to malign the effort or hearts of those who engage in this type of evangelism. But I wonder if we somehow cheapen the gospel by telling people to "just pray these magic words and heaven is yours." The work of real discipleship requires blood, sweat, and tears, not a persuasive argument and a repeatable prayer.

Reaching lost people is clearly *part* of our mission—but how we do it really matters. Too often the end has come to justify the means. Jesus engaged people where they were at, like the woman at Jacob's well, Zacchaeus in a tree, Matthew at his tax collector booth, and many others. (John 4:1-26; Luke 19:1-10; Matthew 9:9-13) Going off road is realizing that the Great Commission in Matthew 28:16-20 is more about our *going* than about their *coming*. Our mandate from Jesus is to seek and to save those who are lost. That means organizing search parties and going to where they are! If you want to reach the lost of our world, you need to meet them on their turf. Yes, it might get dicey and you might find yourself in uncomfortable situations, but over time you will realize they are just people like you in search of something more.

SO WHAT IS THIS THING CALLED LEADERSHIP?

Everybody seems to have an idea. Mine is, "Follow Jesus, obey him fully, and influence others to do the same. When something is right to do, leaders do it regardless of the circumstances." It's about saying *yes* to everything God presents to you. It sounds pretty simple, but that's worked for me over the years.

I love the way Henry Blackaby describes leadership, who in essence says that true biblical leadership always begins with a mission from God that captures the heart and is always bigger than you. I especially love the "bigger than you" part. At the end of the day, we become a leader as we become a servant to HIS mission. One ministry, his, not yours—the ministry of Jesus. You do not need to look for "your ministry"; it's already there. God invites us to join Him in what He is already doing. (These concepts are taken from Blackaby's Spiritual Leadership)

We all have various pieces of His ministry. Jesus is already among the poor, the lost, and the broken as He invites us to join Him there. He might call you to a certain place or group—to the inner city, a church, a school, a country, kids with disabilities, abused women, human trafficking victims, imprisoned criminals, government, or many other people and places. Jesus is already in all those places and calls us to join Him there. **You don't need to start anything because God has already started it.** God was already working in Athens long before Paul got there. When we started our church in Fort Collins, we didn't bring Jesus to Colorado because He was already there at work.

It was so helpful to realize that God was already preparing people we would meet, leaders who would join us, the hundreds who would come into relationship with Jesus for the first time, and the pastors we would send out to plant new churches. For me it took the pressure off trying to make things happen in my own strength. An OG mentor of mine, Murray McLees, once told me, "Make it easy on you and hard on God. Put the pressure on Him and watch him work." This was comforting but also challenging to my type-A, driven personality. So may I suggest stop trying to find "your ministry." There is only one—and it's the ministry of Jesus. He's inviting you to join Him in His mission. Just keep saying *yes* to what's in front of you, and you'll land in the right place.

John Wimber, the founder of the Vineyard movement, said over and over again that our job is simply to do what the Father is doing. Jesus addressed this in John 5:19: "...the Son can do nothing by himself; he can only do what he sees his Father doing, because whatever the Father does the Son also does" (NIV). The key is discerning what the Father is doing and then putting your efforts to that rather than asking God to bless your ideas and vision.

A great prayer? "God, what is it you are doing, and what are you inviting me into?" It might be what breaks your heart and makes you cry. It might be what gets you excited or gets you up in the morning. What is it that you can't stop thinking about? Sometimes it means taking a step toward what never goes away. It just might be God, but you will never know for sure unless you take a step toward it.

When a vision and passion comes back again and again, maybe we need to be like young Samuel who kept hearing his name thinking it was Eli the Priest who was calling him. Eli finally gets what is happening and realizes it was the Lord who was speaking to him.

> *"Go and lie down again and if someone calls again, say, 'Speak, Lord, your servant is listening" (1 Samuel 3:9* NLT*).*

And the Lord indeed spoke to Samuel and changed the trajectory of his life. What a great prayer for every leader that could change your life! "Speak Lord, for your servant is listening," When you get something from the Lord like Samuel did, you lead and move people to God's agenda, not your own. I like that. Without a vision from God, we tend to lead people to ourselves, which is never a good idea. And it never was. Just like Moses led the children of Israel, it's about moving them from where they were to where God wanted them to be. It means laying down your agenda for His. Today, too many powerful visionary leaders show little regard for those they lead. They assume they have to have all the answers, all the vision, and all the next steps. Please don't treat the people you lead like they are expendable; they're not! I hate to be the bearer of bad news, but God isn't concerned about advancing your personal agenda, dreams, and goals.

At the end of the day, leadership is more about building people and fulfilling God's vision rather than building your ministry. And remember leaders go first in everything! As you go, so do those you lead and serve. Bill Hybels often said, "The speed of the leader is the speed of the team," which is so true. It's really hard, if not impossible, to lead people beyond where you are.

All of life's experiences, good and bad, are used by God in the shaping of your leader's heart. God doesn't waste our hurts but uses them to produce His life in and through us. So, embrace your past; the good, bad and ugly, and watch God redeem every piece of it as you give your life away. Your healing may come as you extend a hand that was never extended to you. Giving to others what was never given to you is the ultimate redemption! Take time to examine your heart—and open yourself to the Holy Spirit to examine it for you—take an honest look at yourself and what you are doing and why.

MINISTRY IS TOUGH, BUT SO ARE GOD'S PASTORS AND LEADERS

Too many pastors are not finishing well, and many are not finishing at all. Something has got to change if that is not going to be your story or mine. A friend of mine, James Ryle, said on a number of occasions, "If we do what we've always done, we will get what we've always gotten."

Graveyards are quickly filling up—one for discarded, broken, and demoralized pastors and another for people wounded by them in the process. Bloody and dead sheep are all around. And dead and broken shepherds are right beside them. There has to be a better way.

The call to vocational ministry is a wonderful thing if we can survive it. Yes, it's true that too many pastors are leaving the ministry discouraged, defeated, angry, frustrated, depressed, empty, broken, and disillusioned with it all. Then there are the panic attacks, and nervous breakdowns, addictions, broken marriages, and kids going off the rails that are beginning to be the norm. Some even resort to suicide.

Not long ago, I heard of a young megachurch pastor in California with a thriving church and beautiful family who took his own life. But underneath all that, there was something that was going on that nobody knew about. This is happening much more than you would think. Too many leaders and pastors are in great pain and they see no way out. Nobody seems to notice or care until it's too late. But in the midst of it all, God is raising up amazing leaders who refuse to quit and are standing their ground against the evil one and his destructive plans for humanity. In the following pages, I hope to give you tools to more than survive ministry but to thrive in God's call on your life for the long haul.

YOU ARE UP FOR THE CHALLENGE

In your off-road journey, you will face unprecedented challenges without easy answers. But I believe you are up for it. It takes real courage to lead in today's ministry landscape of political, sexual identity and racially charged conversations. Throw in the threat of mass shootings that we all live under—even in our own churches—and it's a constant battle.

You're forced to wrestle with extreme opinions on the far left and far right and everything in between. You can't keep everyone happy. It's not possible. And everybody seems to think God is on their side, right? It's easy to let political agendas steal the agenda of Jesus and His church. Our post-Christian culture no longer supports and agrees with the teaching of the Bible. The church has too often relied on government and laws to reinforce and support our values, beliefs, and faith. (The church of Jesus has always thrived when the church did not have political power or might.) And to top it off, we have to deal with the madness of Consumer Church and the what's-in-it-for-me mentality of so many Christians today.

These are not problems to run from but to charge into with the love, mercy, and grace of Jesus and His Word. Depending how you look at this, it's a very exciting time to be a pastor as we lead our churches to engage our world looking for real answers from a real God. These are not insurmountable problems, and God has given you an incredible opportunity to make a real difference in the world around us. We have a unique opportunity for the church to rise up and shine in new and fresh ways. And I believe this is a time for the church to be that "city on a hill" for all to see and find hope. (Matt. 5:14)

QUESTIONS FOR THE HEART

1. Is your leadership style more like a cattle driver or a shepherd? Describe!

2. How can you truly know the heart of a leader?

3. Why is a leader's heart important?

4. Do those you lead feel loved and valued by you?

5. How has God used circumstances in your life to shape your leader heart?

6. Who are the leaders in your life that have the heart of a shepherd?

7. Why do people resent being a project? Have you experienced this?

THREE
LEAD FROM THE INSIDE OUT

TYPICALLY, after giving one of my talks (a term I use for sermons) I would fish for some encouragement and ask my wife Becky what she thought of it, hoping she would say it was amazing or not as bad as I thought it was. But typically she would say, "Yeah, it was pretty good and I got something out of it." Pretty good? Come on, I rocked it today. Other times I thought I laid an egg and went to her asking for her opinion, hoping she would say it really wasn't that bad and that she got a lot out of it. What I got was that I was never as good as I thought I was or as bad.

That was until ... I had one of those special Sundays in our fledgling church. It was when everything seemed to click, and a pastor from a large church in Denver called and asked me if I could fill in for him that night. I thought to myself, "You bet—because I have a great talk ready to go from this morning. So, full of self-confidence and with no humility in sight, Becky and I drove the one hour to Denver. And as I stood up to share, I lost it. I could not think clearly, couldn't read my notes, imagined important people in the room who were not there and got totally confused and intimidated.

I knew it was bad, so I did what preachers do. I kept going and going, hoping something good would happen. It didn't! So after it was finally over, I went to Becky to console me and asked this question. "Was I ever worse?" And she said, "I don't think so; I think this was it!" *Oh no, it was really as bad as I thought.* I was devastated and there was no rescue in sight. I blew a great opportunity. I wanted to disappear and tried to avoid people who would lie and say they enjoyed what I had to say. I was looking for the eject button that all pastors wished they had after a really bad sermon. I am not exaggerating when I say it was my worst ever and at the absolutely worst time.

When I could finally laugh about this, I had a picture of God watching this whole mess saying, "Hey, Gabriel, come here and watch this. Rick was dependent on Me this morning, but he doesn't seem to need us tonight so let's see how he does." I think God got a big kick out of all this (I didn't), but my takeaway was that God did not love me any less because of that night. And although it was really bad, He was with me and stood by me to live another day.

When you are at your worst, and you have one of those days, it does not change your value and worth to God. The pay is the same, as a friend once told me. Good, bad or ugly—nothing changes. God won't love you less, and He won't love you more, regardless of how you do. And there are no makeups or extra credit needed in God's Kingdom reality. That was a life-changing moment for me as I not only learned a lesson of what pride can do, but also I am not always going to be at my best and it's really ok. Sometimes I think we need times when we fall on our face to realize that our value and significance are not in how we perform.

There are two questions that ultimately define your life. Who is God, and who are you? You will never truly know who you are apart from knowing God. As you get closer to Him, you begin to discover the fullness of your true identity. Like Paul wrote to the Ephesians, ask God to open the eyes of your heart so you can see Him more clearly. And when you do, you will be able to see who God made you to be.

I believe one of the most powerful ways to lead is from the inside out. Now, what does that mean? Leading from the inside out is not leading by external circumstances but by what God has put inside of you. Too many times I reacted out of my own insecurities in trying to find solutions to situations that I faced. The evil one will throw everything he can to stop you in your tracks and challenge you at your core. You need to be resolved in knowing who you are and what your purpose is. You can't be everything people want or demand you to be. If you do try to please people and give them everything they want, you will not be able to give God what He wants.

It's important to ask yourself these questions:

- Who are you?
- How do you self-identify?
- Is it by your vocation?
- Your accomplishments?
- Titles?
- Education?
- Degrees?
- Race?
- Gender?
- Political or religious affiliation?
- Heritage?
- Child of God?
- Alcoholic or druggie?
- Disabled?
- Divorced?
- Sexual Orientation?

How you answer this is critical to everything you do in life and ministry.

Have you ever looked at a $20 bill and considered where it's been? It might have been used to buy alcohol or drugs; maybe it was even stolen a few times or used for some immoral or unethical purposes. However, its value is not determined by its condition or what it has been through. Its value is determined by its maker, the U.S. Treasury. Likewise, your value is not determined by what you have been through. It was–and is–determined by God. And your worth and value to Him never changes. The bad things that may have happened in your life don't present a problem for Him or disqualify you from reaching your potential.

If you are to have any success on your off-road journey, it is critical to have a true picture of who God is and how He sees you. God wants you to understand: You did not get your identity from your parents. You came through your parents, but your identity comes from God. Maybe you weren't planned by your parents—I wasn't. But that's not the case with God. You cannot afford to allow past failures, the thoughts and opinions of others or even the devil to make you feel devalued. Do not let anyone or anything cause you to believe that your life does not matter or have a purpose. It's a lie. Your purpose flows out of your relationship with God.

LABELS CAN STUNT YOUR GROWTH

I am not a fan of labels. I think labels can be destructive and debilitating, much like having a noose around your neck. They can be something to live up to or down from. I bet you can remember an instance where some of those labels you carried became part of your identity or how you even identify yourself today. I love that God is a "people first" God. He does not see you as your addiction, your sin, or anything else above; rather, He sees you first and foremost as His beloved son or daughter. It's time for those unhelpful labels to go!

One Sunday morning, I taught about labels and gave people an opportunity to go to the cross that we had on the floor, write down a label they did not want anymore, and then attach it to the cross. Hundreds of people responded and wrote something, but one really got my attention. The label was Lesbian. That did not necessarily mean she wasn't a lesbian anymore but that she now saw her true identity as God's beloved daughter rather than her sexual orientation.

Many people will waste their life chasing the wind of trying to find out who they are! You don't have to do that. The challenge—and the most critical part of ministry—is to find your identity, worth, and significance in God alone, apart from what you do.

YOUR WORTH IS FOUND IN WHO YOU ARE, NOT WHAT YOU DO

Who you are in this life isn't summed up by what you do—it's who you are in the depths of your being. Unfortunately, it's easier than you think to lose intimacy with Jesus, even in the midst of great ministry. Leadership and ministry is not where we find our identity or significance, but many search for it there. Your performance and productivity can too easily take the place of God as your source of fulfillment. It was never meant to fulfill the longing of our souls (or to even try to feel good about ourselves). Yet many try. In Matthew 16, Jesus spoke about the futility of gaining the whole world yet forfeiting or losing your soul. Many leaders are doing great things for God but are losing their souls (and more) in the process.

Ministry is a by-product of who you are—always. You can't use ministry to feel better about yourself or fill a vacuum in your life. And whatever you are full of will flow out of you on to the people you lead. If you are full of hurt, you will hurt people. Same with anger, criticism, mistrust, and disloyalty. Rejected people do not promote acceptance. This is why we need to focus on the inside of our hearts, which is the real us, rather than externals.

Jesus put it this way in Luke 6:43-45 (NLT): "No good tree bears bad fruit, nor does a bad tree bear good fruit. Each tree is recognized by its own fruit. People do not pick figs from thorn bushes, or grapes from briers. A good man brings good things out of the good stored up in his heart, and an evil man brings evil things out of the evil stored up in his heart. For the mouth speaks what the heart is full of."

Jesus' preparation for life and ministry was totally based on his identity with his Father—and so it must be with us. He not only knew *what* He was for but also *who* He was. This was critical for Jesus as He faced opposition and challenge to His identity every step of the way, and so will you.

His identity and His relationship with His Father was the foundation for everything He did. His life and ministry flowed from the total love, acceptance and worth He received from His Father. So it must be for us. Without the foundation of love, acceptance, and self-worth from God, we become self-oriented, self-serving, and self-fulfilling leaders. Lacking this foundation of love and acceptance can drive us to use everything and anyone around us to build and establish our identity and self-worth. We can too easily become abusive leaders, using people (rather than building people) to feel better about ourselves.

GETTING OUR IMAGE OF GOD RIGHT

From the Garden until now, God's greatest desire is relationship. Adam and Eve ran from God, and people have been running from Him ever since. Truth is that if you really knew God, you would NEVER run *from* Him but *to* Him! Through Jesus, God finally has caught up with us in a way that deeply connects us to him in relationship. He is the ultimate relentless pursuer! Everything God does is about relationships. It's why Jesus came to the earth in the first place and sacrificed His life on the cross. And brace yourself; it was about more than just dying for our sins and bringing salvation and forgiveness.

Jesus died for a relationship. I believe that Jesus' ultimate mission is not complete until we find our identity as God's beloved child embracing God as our Father. Many of us have opened our lives to Jesus but not the Father. It's a game changer when you realize this. Jesus is the door keeper into the Father's House.

That mission is expressed in John 14:6 (NLT): *"I am the way, the truth, and the life. No one comes to the Father except through me."*

Knowing God as a Father is a critical piece in the life of every leader. For me, the idea of God being a Father was very elusive. I did not know my real dad, and my stepdad was pretty horrible. So thinking about coming to God as a Father was a frightening thought for me. The relationship we have with our earthly fathers can make it easier or more difficult, depending on your situation, to relate to God in a healthy way. These following verses tell us about how we get into God's family and what it means for us.

"Yet to all who received him, to those who believed in his name, he gave the right to become children of God—children born not of natural descent, nor of human decision or a husband's will, but born of God" (John 1:12-13 NIV).

*"God decided in advance to adopt us into his own family by bringing us to himself through Jesus Christ. This is what he wanted to do, and **it gave him great pleasure**"* (Eph. 1:5 NLT, emphasis added).

Through Jesus, you have been adopted into God's family and that gives Him great pleasure. God chose you and me and did the ultimate to make that happen. Adoptions are quite expensive and many have to go to great lengths to make them happen. Yet, God, through Christ, paid the ultimate price to get you and me into His family. It is so liberating when you get this. God chose you to be His son or daughter and paid for you in full. You now live your life as God's chosen child, and this is the foundation of leading from the inside out.

Romans 8:15-17 (NLT) says, "So you have not received a spirit that makes you fearful slaves. Instead, you received God's Spirit when he adopted you as his own children. Now we call him, 'Abba, Father.' For his Spirit joins with our spirit to affirm that we are God's children. And since we are his children, we are his heirs."

"No longer slaves." Chosen and adopted by God—and no longer slaves. Wow! We are heirs to the richest of the richest in the entire universe. How does that sound to you? And we call Him "Abba Father." *Abba* is an Aramaic word of the most intimate expression of the Father in Jewish culture of the day. It is like us calling God "Daddy" or "Papa." This idea of God as a father was a big stretch for me and took time getting used to. The Jesus piece was easier, but the Father part was way more challenging for me. I now love calling God, Papa God, which really works for me and reminds me of the relationship I have with Him. Yet so many lies and distortions persist that keep us away from this Father that Jesus died to bring us to.

One major lie we hear is that Jesus is good, but watch out for his Father. The perception of too many is that Jesus was on a rescue mission to save us from the wrath of an angry, unappeasable Father. I once had a picture of this deception with a scene in heaven where the Father is about ready to blow a gasket because of the awful sin in the world. The Father is shouting with fire coming out of his nostrils, and then He declares, "I promised no more floods, but I have other ideas." But then Jesus shows up and holds his Father back from destroying the world and begs the Father to withhold his anger and offers to come down to the earth and give His life to appease his Father's anger. Reluctantly, the Father, breathing hard, finally relents and says, "But if you're not back in thirty, I am going to destroy them."

This jolting picture is not only false; it's too often the perception that many have of God the Father. But that picture is a horrible lie. Jesus did *not* come to save us *from* the Father but to bring us to Him. Isn't that the essence of John 3:16? For God "so loved the world" that he sent his one and only son to bring us home to him. I had a second picture where the Father is in heaven lamenting how his beloved are destroying themselves and have no idea how much the He loves them and wants to be close to them.

KNOWING GOD AS OUR FATHER

If you want the true picture of what the Father is like, all you need to do is look at Jesus and you will know. Philip approached Jesus wanting to know about this Father that Jesus had been talking to them about: "'Lord, show us the Father, and we will be satisfied.' Jesus replied,

'Have I been with you all this time, Philip, and yet you still don't know who I am? Anyone who has seen me has seen the Father! So why are you asking me to show him to you?'" (John 14:8-9 NLT).

I have a question for you: Who do you find it easier to talk to when you blow it big time? Is it easier for you to go to Jesus? Or do you go to the Father?

Many people of whom I've asked this question find it easier to go to Jesus because of their perception that Jesus is the good, nice, compassionate, and forgiving one, while the Father is quite harsh, quick to punish us, and ready to lower the boom. Many find it easier to go to Jesus because they think they will get a better deal with Him than with that old harsh Father God. This kind of thinking reveals a false perception of both Jesus and the Father. Having a true picture of God is foundational for finding our identity and significance from God.

JESUS' BAPTISM AND THE FATHER'S BLESSING

Mathew 3:16-17 explains that the Father is ready and willing to embrace us with His love: "As soon as Jesus was baptized, he went up out of the water. At that moment heaven was opened, and he saw the Spirit of God descending like a dove and alighting on him. And a voice from heaven said, 'This is my Son, whom I love; with him I am well pleased'" (NIV).

This was a powerful moment in the life of Jesus was when the

Spirit of God descended on Him and the Father spoke His full blessing in this very public setting. But something seems wrong. Jesus had not done anything yet to warrant or deserve this blessing. Right! At this point, He hadn't walked on water, fed the five thousand, raised any dead people, or endured the cross. From our worldly perspective, it seems like this blessing should have come after Jesus finished His mission and went back to the Father in heaven. I can envision all of the heavenly hosts gathered for this special moment of Jesus' arrival. The band is ready and the angels have been practicing for this moment. Then the Father steps up and welcomes Jesus home, declaring, "You are My Son, whom I love. I am pleased with you" (Mark 1:11 International Standard Version).

But this is not the way it went down. Jesus did not have to wait until He was back in the Father's house. He received the full blessing of his Father *before his ministry began.* What? No walking on water? No healing the lepers? No challenging the Pharisees? No raising Jairus' daughter from the dead? No cross or resurrection?

It was from total love and full acceptance that He lived His life and did what the Father called Him to do. Jesus had nothing to prove. He already had it all, like you and I do. What freedom of having nothing to prove to anybody, even God!

Then Jesus' biggest challenge comes. The Spirit of God leads Jesus into the wilderness to be tempted by the devil. The very identity the Father had just affirmed is now directly and forcefully challenged by Satan. So it is with you and me.

The battle of battles is the one for your true identity. It was make-or-break for Jesus right there as the devil went after Jesus' identity. I am paraphrasing parts of Matthew 4:1-11, but essentially, Satan challenged Jesus with, "If you are the Son of God, prove it. Turn these stones into bread! If you are the Son of God, jump off from the highest place of the Temple," and "if you are the Son of God, worship me and I will give you all the kingdoms of the world!" And Jesus would have none of it. The devil came to him at His weakest point and challenged the core of who He was!

If it were me, I would have turned the whole mountain into bread and shoved it up the devil's nose. "You don't think I can do this? Watch this!" But I am not as free and secure as Jesus. Jesus did not have to do the dance we so often do. He was free and knew who He was. Wow, the sound of freedom.

Later, on the Mount of Transfiguration with Peter, James, John, Moses and Elijah, the same affirmation comes once again. (Matthew 17:5) Soon after, Satan goes for it one last time attacking Jesus' identity when He was at his weakest.

Have you ever noticed that Satan tries to do his thing when we are at our weakest and lowest point? Certainly now he can stop Jesus. Anything to get Him off the cross and thwart His assignment from God.

Remember what the High Priest says? "If you are the Son of God, come down from that cross" (Matt. 27:40 ESV). Again if it was me, I might just jump off the cross, slap them upside their heads and then get back on the cross and do my business. "You don't think I can come off this cross? Watch this! Bam!"

I remember a song about how Jesus could have called ten thousand angels to rescue Him. I might have called twenty thousand. But I am not free like Jesus—and neither are some of us. You constantly feel like you have something to prove to justify yourself in this world. You don't!

Instead, Jesus does the unthinkable. "Father, forgive them, for they don't know what they are doing" (Luke 23:34 NLT). Really? It sure seemed like they knew exactly what they were doing. But Jesus forgave them instead. Who does that? Someone who knows who they are and has nothing to prove. Nobody could pull Jesus' strings. He was free to love those who hated and cursed Him. He used His power to love in the face of incredible hatred. So it can be with you if you know who you are and what you are for. Jesus was free to give people what they needed, not what they deserved.

That is mercy. He also told us that those who are merciful will be shown mercy.

When we have our identity in the wrong place, we can become dangerous and have a propensity to hurt and use people for our agenda. Being free and knowing who we are frees us to be what God wants us to be in someone's life. We can forgive and love those who hate us and use us just like Jesus did.

Like so many, I spent much too long working to find my identity and worth—trying to prove myself to most everyone, including coaches, teachers, employers, friends and colleagues. When I met Jesus, I found that what I was looking for I already had. When you move from family to family and have to behave or you're out, that experience can produce deep insecurity and drive a person to please others just to survive. Every family who took me in meant I had to prove myself all over again. I was grateful to every one of these families, but I was never the son, only the kid they were helping, and I wore that stigma for a long time.

Unfortunately, I took that attitude into my relationship with Jesus feeling that I needed to prove myself to Him. It wasn't until I realized God's unconditional love and acceptance that I was able to stop performing and trying to prove myself to everyone around me. Getting to know God as a Father who adopted me through the blood of Jesus has changed my life forever—and I don't have to prove myself to anybody anymore. I feel plenty of emotion as I write this. I wonder what if people might reject what I have to say on these pages. I'm reaching a point where I'm really okay with whatever criticism I receive because this book—like any other venture in my life—it is not going to change who I am or what I am worth. I am only hoping my journey and what I have learned can be helpful to you. When what has happened in your life works out to the benefit of others, it is the redeeming work of God in your life.

When you discover and walk in your true identity, amazing things begin to happen. You no longer have to strive after God's love because you already have it. He says to you what He says to

Jesus, "You are My child (son/daughter), and I love you, and I am pleased with you."

RECEIVING THE BLESSING

The first part of the blessing the Father gave Jesus and wants to give to you is important because God is not ashamed to identify with you: "You are my child! My beloved son. My beloved daughter!"

Once while shopping, I got separated from one of my sons. I heard a call over the public address system, "Will the parents of Greg Olmstead please come to the front of the store?" When I got there the manager said, "Is this your son?" My first reaction before answering was, "What's he done?" Like if he did something bad I was not going to claim him, which was not true. The point is that God lays claim to you no matter what you do, have done, or will do!

The second part of the blessing is important as well: "Whom I love." It's not just any son or daughter, but one whom He loves. One of the biggest obstacles we have is believing that God loves us. Really, it's true. It's why so many prophetic words say over and over again: "I love you, My child." I used to get tired of hearing that, but now I realize that God keeps saying this because we don't really believe it. I live with me every day and can't see why He loves me like He does, but He does. Our identity is who we are —and *whose* we are—not what we do. That's hard in our culture where worth emanates from what we do.

The third part of the blessing is the more challenging part for me. "I am pleased with you." I am not pleased with me so there is no way He is. God is certainly not pleased with everything we do, but He is pleased with us as his sons and daughters.

What I hear is, "Rick, I am pleased with you, not because of anything you do but because you are My son. You bring me pleasure!"

Maybe you have struggled to get affirmation and approval

from your mom or dad, a coach or a teacher. Maybe your best was never good enough or perhaps you felt you could never measure up. You might have been the black sheep of your family, but none of that matters unless you allow others to decide who you are and what you are worth. You may never get it from them, but the beauty of it all is that when you discover that your value and identity comes from God, you become free to live the life God has for you without being chained to what others think!

We need to see ourselves through God's eyes. Our identity is in Him. What He says about you matters more than what people think. You and I have been chosen by God, and none of us is an after-thought to God. I used to feel like I was a kind of afterthought to God considering I was born in adultery, and He was stuck with me. A while ago, I had back-to-back dreams that revealed the lie in how I viewed myself vs. how God saw me.

The first dream was that I heard laughter and people singing, so I peeked in and discovered that Papa God (what I love to call God) was having a gathering with His kids. I was trying to be quiet but Papa God saw me and people turned around, and there I was with all eyes on me. Then God said, "Rick, we were not expecting you but since you are here, why don't you come in and stay for a while?" Grateful, I quickly found a seat in the back and did my best to behave and not bother anybody, which was my M.O.

The second dream was quite like the first. Same place, same laughter and singing, and I peeked in like before but this time something was different. This time Papa God said, "Welcome home, Rick, we are so glad you are here. We were expecting and waiting for you." Everyone was all smiles as I was welcomed into the family I never had.

That was a life-changing moment for me as I had felt tolerated by God but certainly not chosen. It's hard to feel chosen when you know you were born unwanted and messed up people's lives: my mom, my dad, his wife and his family. No way was I chosen to be here; I assumed God was forced to keep me around since I was here. I don't believe that lie anymore. I am just as much God's child as anyone else. We all become God's child as we are born again by the Spirit of God and adopted in God's family. Young leader, you are not an afterthought to God. You are His chosen child and He loves you more than you can imagine!

John 1:12-13 was huge for me: *"Yet to all who did receive him, to those who believed in his name, he gave the right to become children of God,* **children born not of natural descent, nor of human decision or a husband's will, but born of God"** (NIV).

I realized that the cross was God's demonstration of His love and my value to Him. God paid the ultimate price for my adoption into His family...the blood of Jesus Christ. I now know who I am—and have nothing to prove to anyone because God has freed me to live the life He intended for me. You too have nothing to prove to anyone. You have God's total approval. You are worth everything to Him. Like Jesus, we can live and lead from God's love, acceptance and approval.

YOU ARE CHOSEN, YES YOU!

Ephesians 1:4-6 (NIV) says: *"For he chose us in him before the creation of the world to be holy and blameless in his sight. In love he predestined us for adoption to sonship through Jesus Christ, in accordance with his pleasure and will—to the praise of his glorious grace, which he has freely given us in the One he loves."*

Before you were born, God chose you and set forth his purposes for your life. When you see yourself through the lens of God's perfect unconditional love, everything takes on new meaning. He is your Papa God. You don't have to look over your shoulder to see if you have the Father's (God's) love and approval because you already have it. You don't have to climb mountain after mountain trying to prove yourself.

You can hold your head up high and be proud of who you are, and whose you are! You can go for it all because you know God has your back. When you fall (and you will), you can get right back up and go again because Papa God is there to pick you up.

Because you are loved, you can love others, even those who don't love you. You are accepted and you can accept others, and because you are forgiven, you can forgive others. Your life and leadership flows from already having God's love, acceptance and forgiveness, not striving to get it!

And you don't have to perform anymore. Performance is such an insecure thing and an endless trap. As long as you perform well, you get love and approval. But what happens when you don't or can't perform well anymore? Something happens. You get old (like me). You get into an accident, come down with a disease, or tragedy strikes. It is interesting that professional athletes struggle and have a tough time after their playing days are over because their worth was tied up in their performance.

They wonder, "*Who am I now?*" And an identity crisis sets in, causing many to blow up relationships, turn to chemical abuse, experience depression and despair, or they self-destruct. It's one thing to know that God loves you when you are at your best, but it's quite another to know He loves you when you flop. As a pastor, I used to feel like I was only as good as my last sermon, my last counseling moment, funeral, wedding or whatever. Sometimes real change comes through your own personal crash-and-burn moments. I hope you learn from yours when they come like I did from mine. Great relief comes when you don't live with the pressure to perform and live up to an impossible image of who you and others think you should be.

THE BUTTERFLY EFFECT

Lastly, sometimes we seem to have the idea that as a Christian and follower of Jesus, God wants to change us into something "otherly." Yet that goes totally against the idea that we are fearfully and wonderfully made by God as is. It is easy to buy into the lie that God kind of puts up with you until you change and become acceptable to him. God simply wants to transform you more into who you already are and who He has created you to be, like the image of the caterpillar becoming a butterfly.

I wonder if caterpillars have any idea that they are actually butterflies in the making. It might interest you to know that the DNA of a caterpillar is exactly the same as the butterfly they become. The process of growing from a caterpillar into a butterfly is called metamorphosis, which describes the stages of a caterpillar before being transformed into that beautiful butterfly.

That butterfly was always inside that caterpillar ready to someday sprout wings and fly like the wind. So many of us are like that caterpillar—we can't envision being something more than we already are. But God sees that butterfly in all of us and, through Jesus Christ, that metamorphosis takes place. Sometimes because of life and how we see ourselves, the idea of us being like a butterfly is unthinkable.

God wants to free you to be everything He has intended you to be. The caterpillar doesn't have to work at being a butterfly; it will happen as the caterpillar is nourished and grows as it was created to be. You do not have to strive to be what God has called you to be; it's already in you, and God is working on the butterfly growing inside of you. So, we start as that caterpillar but we finish as an amazing and beautiful butterfly!

Put another way: You don't have to try to be somebody because you already are somebody. Knowing who you are and 'whose' you are, frees you to live the life you were always meant to live.

QUESTIONS FOR THE HEART

1. What does it mean to you to lead from the inside out?

2. Where do you get your identity and self-worth?

3. When you think of God as a father, papa or dad, how does that make you feel?

4. Do you feel you have to strive for God's love and affirmation?

5. Do you see yourself as a caterpillar or a butterfly? Explain,

6. Share your most recent "flop" story!

7. What label have you carried that needs to go?

FOUR
NEVER BE ASHAMED OF YOUR STORY

Everyone has a story. And yours is one of the most powerful tools you possess. Sometimes we don't think our story is important because it's not glamorous. You might be convinced that a Hollywood version of your life would have moviegoers asleep before the opening credits even finished. Yet when we hear a story of someone's dramatic conversion where they were molested, shot heroin into their eyeballs, in and out of prison, were the most notorious gang leader in their neighborhood, and then Jesus came and turned their life around—those stories can be intimidating. I have met some people who felt like they needed to go out and do something crazy so they could have a bigger story to tell about what God did in their life. Now, that is crazy!

But perhaps God's given you a different story to tell, which is your story. Maybe you grew up in a family who nurtured you in the ways of Jesus, and you have followed Him all your life. People need to know that following Jesus is not just for a season but for all of life. Your story may be about the faithfulness of God as He fulfills His purposes in your life. Maybe it's overcoming obstacles or making a difference in somebody's life. Your story could well connect with someone whose life experiences are more similar to yours.

My wife Becky struggled at times with her story until she realized that she indeed had a powerful story to tell, which she now shares all over the world.

Her story in her own words:

I grew up in a Christian home and went to church all my life. Sunday morning, Sunday night, Wednesday night, and every other time the church doors were open, I would find myself there. At one point my seven-year-old sister told me that she had given her life to Jesus, and I thought, "That's what I want to do!" So the next Sunday, bored to tears sitting in my pew at an adult Sunday night service, I heard the pastor give an invitation for people to give their life to Christ. I was so excited that I raised my hand but no one acknowledged me, not the pastor, my parents, nor anyone else. I was completely ignored because I was just a child. But not to be deterred, I knelt down in my pew and prayed for Jesus to come into my life after the service. At that moment, I felt a warmth come on me from the top of my head down to my feet. I then got up and went to tell my sister what had happened. That was a life-changing experience, and I have been following Jesus ever since!

Don't you just love this? A seven-year-old girl helped lead her five-year-old sister to Jesus, and they have both followed Him every day of their lives. Today, Becky co-leads a global children's movement and is a huge advocate for giving children an opportunity to give their life to Christ even at an early age like she did. She has written a book, *The Best News Ever*, a reimagined way of sharing the good news of Jesus to children. She has seen hundreds of kids give their lives to Jesus as a result. And all this has come out of her story, a story that she didn't realize for many years would connect with people in the way that it has. Nobody knew how much God was working with that little girl on that Sunday night, but God sure did. And though she was overlooked that night, she has made it her life's mission to make sure that no child is ever overlooked like she was. It's a great example of the power of a story and what it can accomplish.

WHAT'S YOUR STORY?

People need to hear your story, whatever it is, and you need to tell it over and over again. So, what is your story? You are a product of your story, the good, bad and ugly. Your story is also part of God's bigger story and reveals who you are, why you are, and what matters most to you. We are all shaped by our past in one way or the other. Your story is powerful, yet evolving and it's only yours! It's so critical to embrace your story as you discover that you are part of God's bigger story. Your story may be the most powerful tool to share about Jesus, but it can also fend off the lies of the evil one about what God has done in your life. People can disagree with your theology and viewpoints, but they can't argue what God has done in and through your life. Your story is your story. It is also God's story. As you share your story, you will discover that God has always been in your story!

The apostle Paul led with his story almost everywhere he went and told it over and over again. The core of his story is expressed here in Acts 22:3-16 (NLT):

> *Then Paul said, "I am a Jew, born in Tarsus, a city in Cilicia, and I was brought up and educated here in Jerusalem under Gamaliel. As his student, I was carefully trained in our Jewish laws and customs. I became very zealous to honor God in everything I did, just like all of you today. And I persecuted the followers of the Way, hounding some to death, arresting both men and women and throwing them in prison. The high priest and the whole council of elders can testify that this is so. For I received letters from them to our Jewish brothers in Damascus, authorizing me to bring the followers of the Way from there to Jerusalem, in chains, to be punished. "As I was on the road, approaching Damascus about noon, a very bright light from*

heaven suddenly shone down around me. I fell to the ground and heard a voice saying to me, 'Saul, Saul, why are you persecuting me?'

"'Who are you, lord?' I asked. "And the voice replied, 'I am Jesus the Nazarene,[a] the one you are persecuting.' The people with me saw the light but didn't understand the voice speaking to me. "I asked, 'What should I do, Lord?' "And the Lord told me, 'Get up and go into Damascus, and there you will be told everything you are to do.'

"I was blinded by the intense light and had to be led by the hand to Damascus by my companions. A man named Ananias lived there. He was a godly man, deeply devoted to the law, and well regarded by all the Jews of Damascus. He came and stood beside me and said, 'Brother Saul, regain your sight.' And that very moment I could see him!

"Then he told me, 'The God of our ancestors has chosen you to know his will and to see the Righteous One and hear him speak. For you are to be his witness, telling everyone what you have seen and heard. What are you waiting for? Get up and be baptized. Have your sins washed away by calling on the name of the Lord.'"

Paul never forgot where he came from and what Jesus had done in his life, and he shared his story every chance he got. Every time he shared this, I suspect it was an emotional moment as he re-lived his dark past, his encounter with Jesus on that road to Damascus and the call that was to follow.

YOUR STORY IS A WORK IN PROGRESS

Like Paul, Peter, and so many others, you are a work in progress—no finished people need apply. The great news is that God promises to finish what He started. Paul's story evolved as he discovered more of who he was and about the God he now served. There's no need to wait for the finished product; share your story as it develops. And never ever be ashamed of your story, whether it's exciting or seems rather mundane.

There are parts of our story we would like to forget or change if we could. But here's the problem with that. If you could change your past, you would cease being you. Your life experiences have made you uniquely you. For far too long, I didn't realize I even had a story to tell, let alone that I was a part of God's bigger story. Discovering your story may be part of your off-road journey.

In 2011, I had a life-changing encounter with the Holy Spirit at a Global 4/14 Window Summit gathering in Singapore where I felt God calling me to give the rest of my life to being an advocate for this emerging generation. At the end of that encounter, I thought I heard God say, "Rick, your life is about to make sense!" And so it has. Little did I know that years later, my wife Becky and I would be chosen to lead this very Global 4/14 Movement as well as a nonprofit called Generation Now. My time serving as a teacher, coach, and principal have proven to be a valuable asset along with being a pastor for the last forty years. Then when I combine that work experience with my past coming from a very broken childhood, I realize just how uniquely equipped I am to advocate for Generation Now. And if I'm honest about it, I didn't see any of this coming, but God was planning it all along. So it is with you. God works His ultimate plan for your life, using every piece of your story. Sometimes as we go through life, much of it seems to make no sense. But as you watch God work and keep your eyes on Jesus, you will eventually see it all come together. My prayer for you is that even though your life does not make sense right now, you can put your trust in Him, knowing that He has your life in His hands.

Perhaps like some of you, I didn't know I even had a story at first, at least not one worth telling. Looking back, I wonder why I never shared my story in my early years. Deep down, I think I might have been ashamed of it and didn't want people to know. Why tell others about my broken life? I might lose credibility as a young leader. How wrong I was. God has redeemed my life in more ways than I could have imagined, and now I realize that if God isn't ashamed of my story, why should I be?

NEVER BE ASHAMED OF YOUR STORY

I was recently in Uganda and had the privilege of sharing my story in various settings. At the end of our trip, one of the "house moms" who was at one of the services told me that she was deeply impacted by my story and that mine was an "African" story. She went on to say that she had been ashamed of her life and had never shared her story. "But after listening to you, I want to share my story right now with your group." She went on to share a story of unbelievable abuse and abandonment throughout her life, but also how God was faithful to her and miraculously rescued and restored her family. It was powerful and captivating to all of us. Sharing my story unlocked something in her so she would not be ashamed of her story anymore. That is the power and ripple effect of your story. It can free people who have given up on God and life. It gives hope when hope has died. If God did this for you, maybe He can do it for me too!

My story is a tough one to tell, starting with the fact that I was born in adultery. My 19-year-old mom had an affair with a married man with three children. Fortunately, she made the courageous choice not to abort me. But choosing to have me made her life really tough. A few years later, she had a one-night stand with an entertainer and had another child, my amazing sister, Kate. The early years were a blur for me as I only remember faces of those who took care of me while my mom worked.

When I was seven, my mom eventually married for the first time and had two more children, my brothers Mike and Mark. That's when I discovered that sometimes no dad was better than a really bad dad. My stepdad (whom I had the privilege to lead to Jesus before he died) was a professional gambler, and their relationship was extremely explosive and violent; we had the police at our house numerous times. Even at age seven, I was continually left alone unsupervised along with my younger sister. Over the years, my stepdad drifted in and out of the picture. We were continuously moving from one place to another as soon as the money was all gambled away. There were times when we had to make our getaway under the guise of night because we could not pay the rent due the next day, which enraged my mom. All this and more eventually drove my mom to partying and binge drinking.

That marriage didn't last long, reducing our family to just her and us four kids. It also left me as the de facto head of the household much of the time when I was 12. Once I reached junior high, I had attended ten different elementary schools, two of them twice. It was tough continually being the new kid in school. I learned to make friends with the toughest kids in the school for my protection—and it worked most of the time. Survival was my biggest and only goal. But I was a mess, caring for my two brothers and sister, staying up all night, skipping school, and nursing my mom back to health after she returned home drunk some nights, often black and blue from getting into fights. I had no idea that this was not normal family life, but I was becoming suspicious. Still, it was the only life I knew. Social services would've taken us away if they had any idea what was going on. Then something happened that changed the trajectory of my life.

My best friend, Geoff, and his family, the Millers, invited me to come live with them. I went for it and never looked back. Though I felt guilty for leaving, my decision to move in with the Millers meant blowing up the family as my sister went one way, my brothers another (back with their dad), and I had no idea where my mom went.

At the Millers, I experienced a whole new reality that initially was overwhelming. They were a family that had rules and boundaries, things I wasn't accustomed to such as having to go to school every single day. And if you stayed home sick, you really had to be sick. Chores became part of my daily life, and I had to make my bed every day before I went to school. Dinner was held at a specific time, and if you were late, there was no dinner. Weekends started with cleaning my room and working in the yard. The idea of work before play was new for me. Though I chafed under this discipline, I later realized that it was exactly what this undisciplined kid needed. Without the Millers, as hard as it was at times, I don't think I would've made it.

After two years with the Millers, I graduated from a junior high of nearly four thousand students, and a new door opened for me. The family my sister was living with asked me to go with them to visit their parents for the summer in Tehachapi, a town the size of my junior high. It was about one-hundred fifty miles north of LA. At the end of the week, a wonderful Mormon family we visited offered me the opportunity to come live with them on their 650-acre property about fifteen miles outside of this small town. I had no idea why they would invite a boy they had just met into their family, but I accepted their offer. I loved my new family, the Mannings (Harry, Glenda, Chuck and Jeff), right from the start. All this was exciting to me because I knew that my real father and his family were Mormons, which felt like this gave me some inexplicable family roots. Harry taught me to shoot a gun, hunt for squirrels, and drive a truck—all new experiences for this city kid. Two years later, the Mannings decided to move to Florida, and though they offered me the chance to move with them, I didn't feel like I was supposed to go.

Then, out of the blue, another family who heard of my situation and knew I played football, the Johnstons (Spike, Lee, Peggy, Jeff and Annie), offered me the chance to go live with them and finish my senior year of high school. The Johnston's taught me how to ride horses, go on trail rides, and attend church on occasion, all while supporting my many athletic endeavors.

Coming from a large school in the Los Angeles area to a small school of four hundred, I experienced some newfound success. My final summer in Tehachapi, I worked at the local golf pro shop and ended up living with the family of my friend John Davis, the son of the local golf pro. I'd become obsessed with golf by that point, even earning the Most Valuable Golfer award in my high school as I had dreams of becoming a professional golfer.

THE GOD FACTOR

After graduation, I moved back to southern California and started attending Cal State University, Dominguez Hills. My focus there was playing on the golf and baseball teams and not studying, which wasn't the smartest approach. The Vietnam War was ramping up as protests were a daily occurrence on our campus. At that time the draft was by lottery drawings and the list stopped at 138. My number was 146, so I narrowly avoided serving in Vietnam. But my life was totally empty. I was quite lost, devoid of any vision or meaning for my life. I was just existing and trying to survive and embracing whatever moment I was in. It felt like I was on a treadmill to nowhere.

Just as I'd begun to slip into this place of wandering, I had a life-changing encounter with Jesus during my second year of college. It all started when my mom "got religion"—at least, that's what I thought it was. Her life had begun to change thanks to her newfound relationship with Jesus, but I didn't want to hear anything about it, especially from her. My closest friends at the time—aside from my childhood best friend Geoff—were a Reformed Jewish guy, who hated Jesus with a passion, and an avowed atheist who had hating Christians in common. However, as time went on, I couldn't ignore just how much my mom's life had changed. She had stopped drinking, cussing, and fighting. She was also home much more than when I was growing up, and it became obvious to me that something had happened in her life that I should no longer ignore.

After much resistance, I finally agreed to meet with her and a 60-year-old Jewish man named Abraham (Abe) Schneider, who had become, in his own words, "a completed Jew," after giving his life to Jesus Christ. As he began sharing his story, I became captivated. He talked about growing up in a strict Jewish Orthodox family. When Abe was forty, he had a life-changing encounter with Jesus. The fallout from his decision was costly. His brothers physically beat him, his wife divorced him, and his family officially disowned him in a special ceremony, something akin to a funeral. At that moment, I felt really sorry for him that he had to suffer so much for something that wasn't even true.

Almost as if he could sense my disbelief, Abe said, "Rick, I want to read you something from the Bible."

My response was less than inviting. "Well, I don't know anything about the Bible, and I'm not sure I believe any of it." Yet Abe persisted. He started reading a passage I found later to be from Isaiah 53—though he didn't tell me where he was reading at the time. He then asked me who it was referring to in this passage. "It kind of sounds like that Jesus guy," I said, unsure of where he was going.

"Where do you think I am reading from?" he asked.

"I guess from that new part," I said, meaning the New Testament.

Then he showed me it was from Isaiah and added that it was written hundreds of years before Jesus was even born. "And yet you identified the person in this passage as Jesus," he said. This stunned me, and made me start wondering if there might be some truth to what he was saying. Then Abe turned to me and said, "Rick, I want you to pray a prayer."

"Sorry, but I don't pray, and I don't know how, even if I wanted to, which I don't."

But Abe wouldn't let me off the hook. "I want you to pray this prayer one time, 'God, if there is a God and Jesus is your Son and you have a plan for my life, I ask you to show me.'"

I resisted at first but finally relented. "Okay, I'll pray this one time, but not right now, and only because of your story." The next night while working at my night job as a custodian, I finished early and got in my broom closet, sat on my mop bucket, and went for it and boy, was it ever awkward. "God, if there is a God and Jesus is your Son and you have a plan for my life, I need you to show me because I don't believe any of this." I added, "But if you are real, and have a plan for my life I will give my life to you."

Then I added one more piece. "If this is not real, I won't pretend like I see others doing and I won't have anything to do with this Christian thing ever again." After my prayer, nothing happened, but I was ok with it because I did what I'd promised Abe I would do. I went home, went to my classes the next day and forgot all about it.

The next week while I was cleaning one of my classrooms at Cal State Dominguez Hills, I turned around because I thought someone had come into the room but no one was there. At that moment, I felt a powerful presence come over me to the point I could hardly stand up and had to hold on to my dust mop to keep from falling. I then began to see—I'm still not exactly sure how—but my life as a kid appeared right in front of me. As I watched different moments in my life growing up as a boy, I heard a voice say, "Rick, I have been with you all the days of your life"—(which was quite a thought for someone born out in adultery)—"and now I want you to give your life to Me." My next thought was, "Well, who are you?" I'd already forgotten my prayer!

Then I heard the words that would change my life forever: "Jesus!" My next thought was, "*Oh no.*" See, my favorite cuss word—among many—was "Jesus Christ." So, I decided right then and there to give my life to Jesus. I was crying for the first time in my life, but I didn't care. I didn't know a single Bible verse, who Jesus was, or anything that was to come. I left that classroom a new person, and I never swore the name of Jesus again. In fact, I stopped swearing altogether from that moment on, which was no small miracle. Transformed by this encounter, I immersed myself in the Bible, found a church and began sharing the love of Jesus with anyone who would listen.

Looking back, this type of visitation was happening everywhere and became known as The Jesus movement. Those I worked with and the golf and baseball team all saw a dramatic change in my life. I truly felt alive for the first time in my life as

God continually overwhelmed me with His love. I think you could say that He loved me to life! I didn't realize until years later that this encounter was also a call to leadership and ministry. The idea of being a pastor, I assure you, was not even a blip on my radar screen. More on this later!

Since that time, I've had the privilege of sharing this story in over twenty countries. Each time I share, there are three things that consistently occur. First, I get a twinge of shame that comes back on me that I have to fight off. Talking about my past and telling people where I've come from was all quite humbling. The more I share my story, the less the shame gets to me.

The second thing that happens is people become very open to what I have to say. They drop their guards after I let down mine. There's something about coming from a place of messy reality as opposed to pretending to be someone who has it all together. That train left the station a long time ago for me! Single moms especially connect with my story because it gives them hope of what God can do in the lives of their children.

And finally, I realize that my story is not just for others—it's for me too. Telling my story reminds me in a good way of where I've come from and what God has done in my life. It also reminds me of where I might be today if Jesus had not rescued me and come into my life that eventful night at Cal State, Dominguez Hills. I know who I am without Christ in my life—a lost, empty, broken, depressed and futureless man. But God had something more. He found me and gave me a life I had no hope of finding. I am so thankful for the life He has given me. Jesus changed my life forever, and He is still in the life-changing business today. I came to Christ during the first "Jesus Revolution," and I believe another one is coming and may be already here. It's so amazing what can happen when your story meets God's story.

And you have a story, one God wants to use to give hope and change the lives of others around you. Whether you grew up in the church all your life or not at all, had a great family or no family, had a season going off the rails or never strayed, it all matters. God wants to use all the parts of your story in the course of what He has called you to. No story is better or worse than another, so don't apologize. There will be people who can't relate to mine but can to yours and vice versa. God wants to redeem every part of your story, even the darkest and most broken parts—if you don't curse it. Your story is a bridge to help people come into relationship with Jesus and so much more.

Ultimately, you can't forget that your story is the one you have, not the one you wish you had. As you share with people, remember that they don't want more information. What they need most is something real, someone they can relate to, which is what your story offers. They want a faith that moves mountains and is meaningful to real life. Sharing your story also means listening to other people's stories. You need to earn the right to tell people your story in two ways: by unconditionally loving them, showing them you genuinely care, and then inviting them to tell you their story and really listening to it. I have found in almost every instance that if I start with them and ask them about their life, sooner or later they will ask me about mine. The more you tell your story, the better you will get at telling it—and it will change you as well.

So, what's your story? There is a world out there ready and needing to hear it. And nobody can tell it like you.

QUESTIONS FOR THE HEART

1. Why is your story important to tell?

2. Can you remember a time when you shared your story with someone? How did they respond?

3. Can you recall a story that has impacted your life in some way?

4. Why are some people ashamed of their story? Are you?

5. Take some time to begin to write out the stages of your story from the very beginning.

6. Have you ever felt your story was not good enough to tell?

7. How has your story changed somebody else's life in some way?

FIVE
EMBRACE YOUR LIMP

LIMPS COME from life's heartaches and troubles, mistakes you have made, or tragedies in your life or the lives of those you love. They may come from things done to you in your childhood, broken relationships, broken promises, or life's disappointments. Sin and bad choices we make can contribute to our limp. Limps also come with failures and heartaches in life and ministry. People die, fall away from God, divorce, suffer from cancer, and blow up their families. And sometimes as a pastor, you get the blame for it. At the end of the day it does not matter how you got your limp but that you don't let it stop you from saying yes to God because of it!

My limp came mostly from my childhood or lack of one. Broken home, no father, a lost and broken stepfather, raised by a very hurting dysfunctional single mom, and being a street kid who seldom went to school. But I also got a ministry limp. That came from one of my best friends turning away from me, another close friend and partner in ministry dying of cancer at the age of 37, and my worship pastor having an affair with another staff pastor. All this contributed to a pretty significant ministry limp for me even in the midst of great ministry. Another limp came when my son Greg had severe scoliosis and needed surgery that took him out of sports and left major scarring both emotionally and physically. More recently, I got an addition to my limp collection as I was diagnosed with CLL leukemia, which is one more obstacle for God to overcome in my life like He has in all the others.

Some of the apostle Paul's limp came from his past where he hunted down Christians and had them put to death. Another limp would have come from what he called his "thorn in the flesh" that he said tormented him. Whether it was a physical infirmity, persecution or spiritual oppression of some sort, it was part of his limp. He also describes in 2 Corinthians 11 a list of everything that can go wrong does go wrong.

Where did you get your limp? Don't be ashamed of it! I believe it's important for you to embrace it. If you don't have one yet, you will. It's a part of life, and you can't avoid it no matter how hard you try. Jesus told us that in this world, we are guaranteed trouble but be encouraged because he has overcome it. (Read John 16:33.) At the same time, don't be afraid of your limp because out of that weakness, God will manifest His power and grace in your life. The best part of all this is that God gets all the credit when it's all said and done.

And don't forget that your limp is not just for you. Every family has a limp. Every church has a limp. Every marriage has a limp. Even Jesus had a limp, which came about as a result of His upbringing and all the stigma and insults about his birth. "Born of a virgin? Yeah, right!" Then there's the cross. If anything qualifies as a limp, that sure does.

YOU DON'T HAVE TO BE PERFECT

Gone are the days where people expected their leaders to be perfect, which is a big relief for all the leaders and pastors who shouldered the heavy burden of trying to uphold the model of what congregations wanted their pastors to be. However, there are still expectations. This emerging generation wants Christian leaders to be honest, real, authentic and act with integrity, which is pretty much the same thing we all want from our parents. And while we can be those things, there's always a tendency to want to hide our shortcomings, failings and brokenness. Every leader has a limp and you don't have to hide it!

Being a leader does not mean leaving your humanity at the front door. Leaders are not immune from the struggles and heartaches of life. Too many times we try to bury our humanity for fear people might reject us if they see us as weak. Leaders actually feel pain, rejection, and heartache like everyone else does. If you cut me, I bleed just like anyone else. We carry the burdens of so many, but who is there for us? Sadly, for many of us, the answer is no one!

God does not ask you to set aside your humanity any more than Jesus did. He didn't. Remember that moment when Jesus wept real tears at the death of his friend Lazarus? The shortest verse in the Bible, John 11:35 says, "Jesus wept." (Interesting that Jesus' weeping gets its own verse!) He was later overwhelmed with emotion as He was looking over Jerusalem knowing the devastation that was coming. Turning over money changers' tables in the temple again shows Jesus' humanity and emotions, this time some anger. (Read Matthew 21:12-13.)

Again, being a leader or a pastor does not require you to be less than human. Unfortunately, we often feel pressure from others but also from ourselves. A lack of authenticity and transparency can create an unnecessary chasm between leaders and the people they serve. Old school says you can't be close to those you lead or show weakness, or people will take advantage of you. This lie that tells us to hide or deny our pain only results in unhealthy isolation and self-protection.

We love to talk about the highlights of our life, but it is the lowlights that sometimes shape our life the most. It's part of the process of you being you. Do not draw back, be afraid or apologize for your weakness, brokenness or struggles. But deal with it —and your sin as well.

Christy's Story

We live in a day where the church leaders tend to focus more on production and performance rather than on the deeper things Jesus says matter most. As a leader, it is your responsibility not just to do ministry well, but first and foremost, to steward your inner life well. I was great at the former, but lousy at the latter. So, God, in His kindness, invited me into a long journey which taught me to focus on the deeper parts of who I am, rather than what I can build.

Healthy leadership doesn't happen by accident. It's hard, it's painful and oftentimes it's very messy. We don't like mess, especially in the church world. In fact, even though the church is supposed to be like a hospital, few are allowed to bleed. Much of the time, leaders can be too focused on ministry but if they aren't healthy, then what they're building won't be healthy.

Several years ago, one of my closest friends was very worried about me due to all the pressures and dysfunction I was surrounded by. The gift of her friendship was that she was brave enough to hold a mirror up and tell me the truth. One thing I have learned is that if we don't have people in our lives who have the courage to speak truth to us, we won't last.

It's easy to think performance and production equals spiritual maturity. It doesn't! Spiritual and emotional maturity go hand in hand. The only way we grow emotionally is if we have friends who will speak truth into our lives, and we listen and lean into areas where we need to grow.

Growth is painful. Period. God sends people into our life sometimes for a season, and sometimes to walk alongside us through our whole journey. Shame is one of the most powerful weapons the enemy uses to keep people in slavery, and leaders are no exception. In fact, vulnerability is often seen as a weakness when actually it is a great strength. Your willingness to be vulnerable, to know yourself, and to be honest with yourself and others is what makes a good leader great.

In the last several years, I have seen too many leaders quit, blow up, and implode, often leaving a wake of hurt and pain in their wake. They never addressed their struggles. You are first and foremost not leaders or pastors, but human beings. We all have struggles, we all have weaknesses, yet if there is no space or place to admit these things without the fear of retribution, then leaders too often choose to isolate. When you isolate, you become a target for the enemy to wreak havoc.

If you want to see a powerful church, and if you want God to use you in the way He desires, then face your own mental health. How do you deal with rejection, betrayal, loss, and pain? How do you safeguard yourself in not only knowing your weak areas, but allowing yourself to be human? It's not your greatness, nor your gifts, nor your abilities that people really need. They don't only relate to your strengths, but rather to your humanity. And first and foremost, you are a human being loved by God to serve God. Knowing this is what brings freedom, not only to yourself, but it is a gift to those you lead. Most importantly, learn how to be vulnerable. The more you learn about who you are, rather than what you can do, the more open you can be with those you've been entrusted to lead.

Christy Wimber, Former Sr Pastor, Speaker, Church Planting Coordinator

PAUL DID NOT HIDE HIS STRUGGLES

Through Paul's letters, you see that he sometimes receives some backlash from certain people who are challenging his motives. Then he opens up about his struggles and weaknesses. He takes the risk and lets them inside.

In 2 Cor. 11:24-30, we read:

Five different times the Jewish leaders gave me thirty-nine lashes. Three times I was beaten with rods. Once I was stoned. Three times I was shipwrecked. Once I spent a whole night and a day adrift at sea. I have traveled on many long journeys. I have faced danger from rivers and from robbers. I have faced danger from my own people, the Jews, as well as from the Gentiles. I have faced danger in the cities, in the deserts, and on the seas. And I have faced danger from men who claim to be believers but are not. I have worked hard and long, enduring many sleepless nights. I have been hungry and thirsty and have often gone without food. I have shivered in the cold, without enough clothing to keep me warm. Then, besides all this, I have the daily burden of my concern for all the churches. Who is weak without my feeling that weakness? Who is led astray, and I do not burn with anger? If I must boast, I would rather boast about the things that show how weak I am.

Here Paul gets pretty raw with his emotions and frustrations and gives it to us straight. After defending himself, he addresses his suffering and then gets personal about his life's struggles. As rewarding as ministry can be, it is still full of difficult times, hardships, heartaches and strife—and Paul lets it all out here.

In Romans 7, Paul again talks about his personal battle with sin: "For what I want to do I do not do, but what I hate I do" (Rom. 7:15 NIV). Then, a few verses later, Paul asks, "Who will rescue me from this?" (Rom. 7:24 NIV). (Can you relate?) He answers his own question in Romans 8:1-2 (NLT): "So now there is no condemnation for those who belong to Christ Jesus. And because you belong to him, the power of the life-giving Spirit has freed you from the power of sin that leads to death."

Paul acknowledges his struggles and weakness but also that the power of the Holy Spirit has freed him from the power of sin. When we share our struggles, we also get to share and celebrate the victories.

Paul told his disciple Timothy that he was "the worst of sinners" (1 Tim. 1:16 Good News Translation). Making a statement like that today can get you fired quickly from your ministry or church. Obviously, Paul was a bit hard on himself here and probably exaggerating a bit, but he felt it was important to share how he felt to his young disciple, Timothy. OG's, can you imagine mentoring a young leader and telling them you are the worst of sinners? Wow! Mentoring is letting people into your life!

As leaders, when we experience these emotions and situations, where do we turn and who can we go to when we hurt? When we struggle? When we want to quit? (You will want to quit many times if you haven't already thought about it.) When you don't know what to do? When you have problems in your marriage? When you have a crisis of faith? Who do you call when you are not okay and need help? Who is there for you? I believe you not only need mentors but also pastors and spiritual fathers in the Lord to guide you in challenging times.

Even shepherds need a place to turn to. And here's the thing: We are not only shepherds, but we're also His sheep. The stats on pastors and depression, pornography, anxiety attacks, affairs, and alcohol abuse are startling. At the end of the day, you only have grace (strength and power from God) to be you, not somebody else. You only have grace to be and do what He has called you to do, not grace to do whatever you want or to be who everyone expects you to be. We all "hit the wall" at times, and when that happens, my advice to you is to step back and stop hitting your head against it.

LEADING WITH A LIMP

When we reflect on the numerous stories in the Bible, we need to consider this question: Who are the people God uses? The rich and famous? The powerful? The put-together, straight-laced characters? Not a chance. You'll be hard-pressed to find more than a half-dozen people characterized as such in the Bible.

Look at the twelve disciples Jesus chose. Certainly he could have done better than them, right? Where is His dream team? Couldn't Jesus find someone besides these nobodies? It seems like it would've been easy for Him to go to the high priests and ask them to give Him their finest and brightest young men to be His disciples. That may be how it works in our world today, but it was not Jesus' way or his strategy. Most of those God called felt unqualified for the task. Gideon, Isaiah, Nehemiah, Peter, and even Moses after forty years in the woodshed of Midian. All of them saying at one time or another, "I can't do this! Find somebody else!"

I have not found references in the Bible where God asked someone if they are capable to do something—but He does ask if they are willing. The question God is asking you, is not *can* you, but *will* you

The truth is that we can actually be too strong for God to use but not too weak *if* we give our weakness and brokenness to God —and then say yes to whatever He asks. Over and over again, God chooses ordinary people to do extraordinary things. And guess what, He gets all the credit. As I mentioned earlier, I love the fact that the Bible does not hide the weaknesses and failures of its characters. The key to who God chooses may be more about who is *available* rather than who is *capable*. God is not looking for superstars but for ordinary regular people who are willing to say yes. We read in Acts 4:13 (NIV): "When they saw the courage of Peter and John and realized that they were unschooled, ordinary men, they were astonished and they took note that these men had been with Jesus."

And in 1 Corinthians 1:26-29 (NLT):

Remember, dear brothers and sisters, that few of you were wise in the world's eyes or powerful or wealthy when God called you. Instead, God chose things the world considers foolish in order to shame those who think they are wise. And he chose things that are powerless to shame those who are powerful. God chose things despised by the world, things counted as nothing at all, and used them to bring to nothing what the world considers important. As a result, no one can ever boast in the presence of God.

I love the fact that the apostle Paul refused to pretend and wear a mask. Like Peter, what you see is what you get with Paul. He refused to posture himself to impress anybody—and you don't need to either. If you follow Paul's life, you quickly see that showing his weaknesses did not hinder him from fulfilling God's call on his life or diminish his spiritual authority as an apostle. He found the secret: The authentic Paul gave the gospel more power, not less! So it is with you. The real you, not the ideal you, gives the gospel more power not less.

You don't have to hide or be afraid of your weaknesses or struggles. You don't have to pretend or wear a mask around people you lead. They may want to put one on you, but don't do it because before long the "masked you" and "the real you" get obscured and you don't know which is which. Refuse to fear being transparent with your weaknesses as they could actually become your strength!

Leading with a limp can actually qualify rather than disqualify you for leadership and ministry. John Wimber famously said, "Never trust any leader who doesn't walk with a limp." I have a hard time trusting a leader who has not been broken—and neither should you. A limp is more of a qualification for a leader than a glowing resume. When I interview people for various positions, I am not easily impressed with all their great achievements and accolades. I take a step back until I can find that limp in there. A leader who is not broken can sometimes be dangerous and even abusive.

Humility and transparency is too often a missing ingredient in leadership today. When a leader wears a mask, so do the people they lead. The real you is always the best deal for everybody. Remember: God opposes the proud but gives grace to the humble!

TURNING A LIMP INTO TRIUMPH

Scott Hamilton

Scott Hamilton, the world-renowned figure skater, was born with a brain tumor. But he didn't know that. At the time, the family thought he just had trouble with his pituitary gland, causing his stunted growth. For four years, Scott was in and out of hospitals. Finally, a doctor told the family to go home and let Scott live a normal life. Looking for something he could do, his parents took him to an ice skating rink. Scott found skating was something he could do. It was fun and for whatever reason, Scott began to grow again. In the meantime, he became the best at what he did. The rest is in the record books. Scott Hamilton became one of the best-known skaters of all time, because he had a weakness that kept him from doing much else. Later, Hamilton was diagnosed with testicular cancer, from which he recovered. Years later, he also faced a brain tumor diagnosis, for which he underwent surgery in 2010 and recovered yet again. He then started the Scott Hamilton CARES Initiative in 1999, with an emphasis on funding cancer research, sharing online information on chemotherapy and providing one-on-one mentorship for patients. **Scott refused to let his limp stop him!**

Bethany Hamilton

Bethany Hamilton had her arm bitten off by a shark. Hamilton started surfing when she was just a child. At age 13, an almost-deadly shark attack resulted in her losing her left arm. She was back on her surfboard one month later, and two years after that, she won first place in the Explorer Women's Division of the NSSA National Championships. Talk about determination. Rather than defeating her, her limp propelled her into new accomplishments. On her social media page, she wrote: "Life is not perfect, but we can adapt through the challenges and 'so called' impossibilities! My ultimate goal in life is to serve God & do well in what he has called me to do."

Rick Warren has said over and over again that "God never wastes a hurt" and it's so true. Romans 8:28 is in play here. *"And we know that God causes everything to work together for the good of those who love God and are called according to his purpose for them"* (NLT). Did you catch that? God causes everything, not some things, to work His goodness and His purposes in your life regardless of the circumstance. When you go through the fiery furnace of suffering and pain, you come out on the other side as fine gold. God promises to refine you; He is the great refiner! He says, *"I have refined you, but not as silver is refined, Rather, I have refined you in the furnace of suffering"* (Isaiah 48:10 NLT).

QUESTIONS FOR THE HEART

1. What are your greatest strengths? Weaknesses?

2. Is it easy or hard for you to share your struggles with others? Explain.

3. Talk about a time when you had to overcome a weakness or heartache in your life.

4. What limp do you currently carry? How are you dealing with that?

5. How has your limp propelled you forward, stopped you or pushed you backward?

6. Do you believe that your weaknesses can qualify you rather than disqualify you for ministry? Explain.

7. How has God used one of your lowlights to make you the person you are today?

SIX
STRIVE TO BE A LEADER WORTH FOLLOWING

As you go off road, think about what kind of leader you want to be. Unfortunately, in our world today, having good character is not a trait many people find necessary in a leader. A quick glance in the political arena makes this evident. But it's your character that makes you a leader worth following. Our standard of leadership is not comparable to what we see in the world around us. Leaders who are committed to maintaining their character will often say *no* to what many would perceive to be an opportunity of a lifetime. They don't pretend to live in two worlds. There is no discrepancy between their public and private lives.

Leaders worth following do the right thing because it is the right thing to do, regardless of the cost, even knowing that doing the right thing can impede their forward progress.

CHOOSE CHARACTER OVER GIFTING

Character is the will to do what's right even when it's hard and goes against the grain. There are times you have to swim upstream against the current of public opinion, where you don't pretend to live in two worlds. To be a leader worth following, there must be alignment between the values you teach others and the values you live out in your everyday life.

For instance, Job in the Bible talked about making a "covenant with his eyes," which is a good example for us to follow so we don't fall into the evil one's traps! (Job 31:1) I think we might also consider making a covenant with our mouth. The Lord cares what comes out of our mouths, which can reveal the condition of our hearts and derail our character. Jesus said it's what comes out of your mouth that defiles you (Matt. 15:11), and James reminds us how important it is to tame or control what we say. James 3:10 says, *"Out of the same mouth come praise and cursing. My brothers and sisters, this should not be!"* (NIV).Many influential and gifted leaders have lost credibility in this arena as they say one thing in public and another in private.

I have noticed an increase in the use of the F-bomb by some well-known leaders. I don't get it. One minute they're on stage with one persona, and off-stage, it's a whole different ball game. If it's not okay on stage, what makes it okay and acceptable off stage? I understand there are certain things we do that are more appropriate in some settings but not in others. I do wonder where Ephesians 4:32 comes into play in all this: *"Don't use foul or abusive language. Let everything you say be good and helpful, so that your words will be an encouragement to those who hear them"* *(NLT)*. Before I started following Jesus, I also understood this duplicitousness, knowing when it was okay to use certain salty language and where it wasn't.

This behavior created no tension in my life until that eventful night at Cal State Dominguez Hills when I met Jesus for the first time—and whose name was my favorite swear word at the time. *What am I going to do?* I quickly realized that using "Jesus Christ" as a swear word had to go, but what about the others like the F-bombs? The duplicity seemed like too much of a burden to bear, so I decided that the F-bombs (and a few others) had to go since they did not fit this new life I now had in Jesus.

I understand that the marketplace and social media dictates

much of what we find acceptable, but that doesn't necessarily make it ok for you or me. Do we use swear words in our prayer life? Why not? I guess my concern is that we are not one thing here and another there because sooner or later we forget which is which. As you grow in your authority and influence, your words matter, and even have more power to build up or tear people down. When you think about the words you use, are they helpful or not ? Take some time and consider the ramifications of this issue in your life and ministry as you talk to God and draw your own conclusion.

Leaders gain followers in many ways. Not all are great. Dictators gain a following. So do cult leaders, criminals too. But they are not worth following. Leaders abound who have large followings but have bad character and are not worth following when you look at their lives. We see this all around us in business, government, and yes, sadly even in church circles. Some of the most successful Christian leaders by the world's standards have terrible character and little integrity. Many times we give them a pass because of their gifting, personality, charm, and accomplishments. If we don't tend to our character, we can easily become one of them.

We are all susceptible to becoming corrupted by our own success if we are not careful. This is especially dangerous and a huge trap for super talented and gifted leaders. I am reminded of Jesus' words: *"For everyone to whom much is given, from him much will be required"* (Luke 12:48 NKJV). The more successful by God's standards you become, the bigger target Satan has on your back! And the more people will be devastated if you fall. It's why we need to stay close to Jesus and draw our life from Him rather than our ministry.

THE SUSTAINABILITY OF CHARACTER

Gifting might launch your ministry, but it's your character that sustains you, ultimately giving you credibility and influence. And it has a much longer shelf life than all your gifting and talents, which wane over time. Your giftedness may open doors, but your character will determine what you will do once those doors are opened. However, we have a tendency to be highly impressed with extremely gifted people. When we become so enamored with a person's gifting and/or charisma, we tend to excuse their sin, arrogance, and bad character. We do not do these super gifted people a favor when we let that giftedness blur our view of what matters most.

The fact that people choose to follow you or me is not necessarily an indication that we *deserve* to be followed. I remember a very anointed and gifted worship writer and leader who was in great demand for worship nights and concerts. The problem was that although on stage everything typically went incredibly well, he would leave a devastated band and sound team in his wake because of his harsh treatment of them. Despite his shortcomings, he would get invited back again and again because he was so good at what he did. There was no doubt he was anointed when it came to leading worship. But was it worth it?

So, what do you want to be remembered for? How talented and gifted you are? How many people you led in worship or have spoken to? How many young adult or college groups you have led? The large crowds who cheer you on or buy your songs or download your teachings? How many Facebook friends you have? Or how many have read your blog? Your credentials or accomplishments? How many big churches you get invited to?

It takes a commitment on our part to work on our character and inner life as much as on our ministry skills. I have seen too many leaders hit the limelight too early ahead of their character development and end up a disaster. It is on the mountaintop of success that too many leaders abandon the convictions and humility that got them there. Jesus once told his guys, *"And what do you benefit if you gain the whole world but lose your own soul?"* (Mark 8:36 NLT). **You might gain success and fortune, but is it worth the cost of losing your integrity, family, and self-**

respect? The answer is a resounding *No!* I recently watched a new movie about Elvis and was struck at the end by the fact that though he was incredibly rich and famous with the world at his fingertips, he died entrenched with such painful and deep regret. This can happen to any of us if we are not focused on what really matters most.

I always wondered about something: **Does crisis reveal or create character?** I think it can be both, depending on how we respond. When you are under pressure, the real you comes out. You can try to control it, but eventually, what is inside comes to the surface. What we say, especially during hard times of stress and anxiety, reveals our truest beliefs and state of mind. Our words unveil our fears, doubts, sarcasm, anger and inner battles, which may point to deeper struggles and expose our need of healing and attention. Refuse to hide or camouflage those true feelings when they come. Listen to your heart and tend to your soul. Invite Jesus into those moments and don't hold anything back. He is able to strip away what doesn't fit when you don't hide your areas of weakness, anger, frustration, unbelief and pain.

I have been in hard situations when I did not like what came out of me and how I responded. My response revealed something was wrong, but it was also an opportunity to grow if I was willing to deal with it. My wife Becky once challenged me with, "Why are you so angry?" My typical male response was, "I'm not angry," but I was and I didn't know why. This confrontation eventually became a huge breakthrough as I was forced to face the anger head-on or watch it destroy my family, marriage, and ministry. I also found myself at times talking to Becky at home differently than I would around people at church which was so dishonoring to her. Who I was at home was not matching who I was at church, and I needed to deal with the discrepancy. I made a conscious choice to work at treating Becky at home the same as I would treat people at church or in any public setting. When you let the little things go, they become big things and eventually eat away at your character.

BEWARE! CHARACTER IN DANGER

Have you noticed that many leaders start off well but unfortunately fall into traps and compromises along the way? Taking shortcuts, winning at all costs, and taking people for granted are just a few of the landmines. Satan will seduce you with everything imaginable to ruin your character. When you lose it, it is really hard to get it back.

Satan has three main weapons he typically uses to take us out as leaders: money, sex and power in no particular order. Most people don't lose their character overnight but over a period of time, like the frog in the kettle analogy. If you put a frog in a kettle with cold water and heat it gradually, the frog will stay in and get cooked to death. On the other hand, if you throw the frog into a boiling pot of water, it will immediately jump out and try to get away. It's the little things we let slip by that set us up for an integrity crash. Some say, "Don't sweat the small stuff," which is crazy and ridiculous. I say, "Sweat the small stuff before it becomes 'the big stuff' and takes you out."

Power. There is a proverbial saying from the English historian Lord Acton, *"Power tends to corrupt; absolute power corrupts absolutely,"* which conveys the idea that as a person's power increases, their moral sense diminishes. I've found that to be true much too often. The more power you have, the less approachable you can become and have fewer people who can or will tell you the truth. Be careful because power can be addictive and the more you have the more you want!

Money. Many leaders have fallen over the issue of money. Don't be one of them! This is an area where it's easy to cut corners and get trapped in practices that are questionable. It was important to me to have as many things in place as possible to keep me accountable with the handling of our church finances. We not only had an outside church accountant and a legal church board, but we also established a financial advisory council that made sure everything we did was financially correct. Finally, any financial benefit to me had to be approved and authorized by our board, which set my salary, benefits, etc. I tried to put as many layers of accountability in place as I could. Doing this was for my own protection, as well as the protection for our church and those I served. As you go on your off-road journey, make sure you put in place strong financial practices early on and add to them as you grow.

On a personal level, how you handle your personal money matters too. Debt is not your friend, and you should avoid it at all costs. Becky and I went deep into debt launching our new church in Fort Collins, and it took years to dig out. We are now enjoying the freedom of being out of debt for the last twenty-five years. Wait for God to provide and live within your means with God's provision! Financial accountability is your friend.

Lastly, when it comes to money, don't be a hypocrite. I often hear leaders admonishing the people they lead to be generous and give sacrificially, but they don't always do it themselves. You don't tell people to put God first with their money and resources if you are not doing the same.

Sadly, I have known some pastors who, although they get their salary through the giving of their people, give little themselves. Financial stewardship is about you putting God first with your money as you lead the way with your giving and your generosity. This giving thing did not come naturally to me as I grew up quite poor and our family did not have an ounce of generosity. We were the takers of this world, fully entitled and without a thought of giving to anybody. Giving and generosity was a journey and a learning process for me. It started with giving something, then working up to giving the tithe, the first ten percent of my earnings, and then giving another ten percent on top of that to various groups. My wife Becky, who grew up in the church, was my tutor and example, teaching me that we never lose by putting God first with our money and being generous. The more we gave, the more God seemed to bless us, financially and other ways as well.

As time went on, whenever we asked for a special offering at our church, Becky and I would always confer because we were committed to personally giving to every endeavor we presented to our church. (That helped us to not have too many special offerings!) I have found generosity to be a good antidote to the stronghold money can have over you. And it can also break the "spirit of poverty" over you and your church or organization as well. Be the leader of your church or organization in generosity.

Sex. After power and money, a third trap that the evil one sets for you is the ambush of the "other woman" or the "other man". Sooner or later, Satan will try to plant someone in your path that "appears" to be everything that your spouse is not, and convince you that you should have what you don't have. Entitlement is such a subtle trap and it hounds us all, lying to us about what we don't have or are missing out on and what we deserve.

The saying that "the grass is greener on the other side," which evolved from a 1920's American folk song, is a reflection of this kind of entitlement. But why is grass green at all? Because someone watered it! The grass is greener where you water it, and that is especially true in relationships. Physical affairs typically begin as an emotional affair that seems innocent enough but escalates when you don't stop it early. One of the biggest traps is believing that it can't happen to you. You need to stay vigilant and on guard to the schemes of the evil one.

Becky and I have an understanding that if either one of us is uncomfortable with the other being around someone of the opposite sex, we stop and back away. We had a woman pastor on staff who Becky told me that she wasn't comfortable with me getting too close to. As we had previously agreed, I backed away, and not long after that, this woman unfortunately had an affair with another pastor on staff.

Trust your spouse and close friends' warnings and instincts when they sound an alarm about something that could destroy your character, marriage or ministry. Do everything you can to guard and protect it, and like the shepherd who guards the sheep pen door from the lurking wolves, do the same. Remember this: **No one will fight for your marriage more than you!**

FOCUSING ON YOUR INNER LIFE

To be a leader worth following, you must give attention to your inner life as much as your outer life. When leaders don't succeed, character often seems to be a major cause. To be a leader worth following, there must be alignment between the values you teach others and the values you live out in every facet of your life.

As you progress in your leadership, focus on your character, work on you, not just what you do. Find a good spiritual director or counselor whom you can meet with regularly. Establish good accountability relationships. Balance your inner life and your outer life. Find someone safe to talk to before your life gets out of balance. Only you can intentionally work on your character. No one else can do that for you.

However, becoming a leader worth following is not a ladder to be climbed in isolation. You can't do it on your own. It's a true partnership between you and the Holy Spirit. It is a working out of your salvation with fear and trembling. It's a joint effort with you and God. God is not going to do this *for* you, but *with* you.

LIVING BY THE SPIRIT'S POWER

We can't talk about character without looking at what Paul says in his letter to the Galatians contrasting our sinful nature/self-effort and the fruit of the Holy Spirit. Chasing after your 'image' or living for it can hinder the development of your character. The key to good character is right here in Galatians 5:16-23 (NLT, emphasis added) which needs little commentary:

> *So I say,* **let the Holy Spirit guide your lives. Then you won't be doing what your sinful nature craves.** *The sinful nature wants to do evil, which is just the opposite of what the*

Spirit wants. And the Spirit gives us desires that are the opposite of what the sinful nature desires. These **two forces are constantly fighting each other***, so you are not free to carry out your good intentions. But* **when you are directed by the Spirit,** *you are not under obligation to the law of Moses.* **When you follow the desires of your sinful nature, the results are very clear***: sexual immorality, impurity, lustful pleasures, idolatry, sorcery, hostility, quarreling, jealousy, outbursts of anger, selfish ambition, dissension, division, envy, drunkenness, wild parties, and other sins like these. Let me tell you again, as I have before, that anyone living that sort of life will not inherit the Kingdom of God.* **But the Holy Spirit produces this kind of fruit in our lives***: love, joy, peace, patience, kindness, goodness, faithfulness, gentleness, and self-control. There is no law against these things!*

Did you notice that it's the Holy Spirit that produces this kind of fruit in your life? When you read this list, which of these traits are evident in your life? I think we all have a mixture since we are works in progress. Like you, I want more of the fruit of the Spirit and less of the sinful nature/flesh stuff. Yet moral purity and the like needs to be something we continue to strive for and not give up on.

I know many Christian leaders who have given up on their fight for moral purity, especially in the sexual arena. That's tragic for sure, but maybe giving up is not such a bad idea. Let me explain. When I give up (not give in) to what I can't do and overcome, that can open the door to what only God can do. That is, if I dare to acknowledge my struggle and invite Him into it, I resolve to get the help I need to win the battle. It also requires getting the help you need whether it's getting prayer, counsel, going to detox/rehab, AA, cutting off the porn or whatever. Just do something and stay in the battle as you rely on the Holy Spirit to work His healing and freedom in your life. And like I said before, asking for help may be the bravest thing you will ever do! It might feel like this does not relate to you in your current season of life. But it will. So deal with your stuff early before it becomes a deeper problem.

ACCOUNTABILITY IS YOUR FRIEND

Nobody is responsible for your accountability but you. It's on you whether you let others into your life and are willing to tell them the truth about how you are really doing. Only you can choose to listen to the voices of concern for you. Only you can make the choices needed for change. You can be in ten accountability groups and still not be accountable! We sometimes forget that we are to be first accountable to God—who sees all—for our lives and ministry. At the same time, we need people in our lives to walk beside us even as we walk with them. The "me and God is all I need" attitude sounds great but doesn't work. God made us to need people in our lives, and God alone is not enough. Sorry! You need both God and people in your life if you are going to make it to the finish line. We need someone who will help us not be stupid and destroy our lives with wrong choices.

But we also need people who have our backs and remind us who we are and what God has spoken over us. We need those who are praying and rooting us on, no strings attached. Accountability is a must in the life of every leader, but it goes two ways. It seems like most of the time when we talk about accountability, the conversation slides to the negative side. I need people to remind me who I am, what God has given to me and His call on my life.

I think that's called intercession. Every leader needs intercessors on their behalf if they are going to do long-haul ministry and not be taken out. David needed a Jonathan, Paul needed a Barnabas, and Timothy needed a Paul. Do you have someone like that in your life?

We all need people who can and will speak truth in love to us. Yes, you need people who have your back. God in front and friends right beside you, friends who not only speak into your life but also lend a listening ear with whom you can share your dreams, fears, and struggles. It's essential to have someone in your life who can see what you can't see. But at the end of the day, you and you alone are ultimately responsible and accountable for your life. **You are only as accountable as you allow yourself to be.**

At the same time, it's helpful to have someone who will actually hold you accountable as much as possible. You can say you are accountable, but are you really? Have you given someone total permission to speak into your life without recoiling? Someone in whom you confide the good, the bad and the ugly? Someone who knows it all? You may have more than one, but it's critical to have at least one. I've heard it said that if you are accountable to everyone, you are actually accountable to no one and I think it might be true.

One example is, sadly, in the life of a megachurch *pastor* who actually did have an *accountability group. But when the chips were down, he had a secret life* that he didn't share with the group. *He had help right next to him but chose another path and lost it all!*

Our struggles with sin and temptation are real, and we should not feel ashamed to let someone in. In fact, it is a risk we must take if we do not want to fall. Pastors are probably the worst because we assume no one will understand and they will reject us. And sadly, they are not completely wrong. Pastors are human, as I have said before, which is not a license to sin but a reality. *Who can you turn to before it's too late?* Pastors need a safe place to share the struggles and temptations they are dealing with. It's critical if we are going to turn the tide.

The bottom line here is that we need to find at least one person we can tell any and everything to—even the stuff that's difficult to admit. We should be able to talk with them about stuff from the past *and* what's going on now. I have that person now, and it's been life changing. Who is this person (or persons) in your life? Your spouse? A friend? Colleague? Counselor? Spiritual director?

So humble yourself and ask for help. James 4:6 reminds us

that God opposes the proud, but He gives grace to the humble, remember? Do it! Take responsibility for your life and ministry.

- Porn? Get help!
- Chemical abuse? Get help!
- Marital issues? Get help!
- Temptation? Get help!
- Anger or depression? Get help!
- Suicidal thoughts? Get help!

Let people in and take off the mask. Tell somebody before it's too late, and it destroys everything you believe in and hope for.

QUESTIONS FOR THE HEART

1. Do you believe character is more important than gifting? Why or why not?

2. Which traits that Paul described in Galatians 5 are evident in your life?

3. What words describe what you want to be known for?

4. Choose one character quality you want to work on and share that with someone who will come alongside you in this journey.

5. Are you working on your "inner life" as much as you are your "outer life"? Would people who know you well agree?

6. Are there areas of gifting you have been relying on rather than your character?

7. Is "profanity" an issue for you? Why or why Not?

SEVEN
JUST SAY YES!

"When you get into a tight place and everything goes against you ... never give up then, for that is just the place and time that the tide will turn." –Harriet Beecher Stowe (1811-1896), American abolitionist

I HAVE HAD many yes moments in my life and ministry—and I've missed a few too. These moments don't get any easier because each time it comes down to this: Will I trust God once again and say *yes* to what I can't do but only He can? Or will I look at the situation and say *no* and walk away? There are divine appointments that only God can fulfill. Sometimes, people will sit around waiting for their perfect situation or offer to arrive. It's imperative that we move beyond our wishful thinking and say *yes* to our reality, one that will end up being richer and more exciting than we could've ever imagined.

I have been a leader in a movement, church planter, pastor of a large church and pastor of pastors, but early on there were few signs that leadership was in the cards for me. Growing up, I have no memory of leading anything or people looking to me to lead, —perhaps because as a kid I seldom spent much time in one place before getting uprooted. It wasn't until my senior year of college at Vanguard University (Southern California College at the time) that two events awakened the idea that leadership may be a part of my life.

The first one was when I went on a senior trip to northern California and ended up in San Francisco for a night. Bill, a friend of mine who was a leader I admired, invited me to go for a run like we typically did back at school. During our run, we came across an African American man who was lying in the gutter. I assumed my friend Bill would stop and help the man but he ran on by. I did too at first. But then it hit me that God was prompting me to go back and check on that guy. I said, "Bill, we need to go back and check on that guy and help him if we can." So, back we went. We took him off the street and sat him back against a storefront wall before we realized he was in much worse shape than we first thought.

He was incoherent and missing one arm. He must have been a mainstay in the area as people continued to walk by without giving him a glance. So we began praying for him when two car loads of Black Panthers drove up and quickly surrounded us. They started questioning why we were there and what were we doing this man. Two white college kids in sweats hovering over this destitute black man—it wasn't a good look. To say I was scared to death at that moment would've been an understatement. I stammered as I explained why we were there, trying to help these gang members make sense of our presence. I could tell they were surprised—shocked actually—and they took a step back after hearing my explanation. Then they said, "We will take it from here with this guy, but you need to get out of here right now because it's getting dark and it's not safe for you white guys to be here." So, with their personal escort, we went off and a seed of leadership was born in me for the first time as I said *yes* to what I thought God was asking me to do.

The second one occurred around Christmas time when about a hundred people or so had spontaneously gathered in the lobby of our dorm and people began singing Christmas carols. Something happened as the Holy Spirit showed up in a powerful way, and the gathering turned into worship and ministry time. I was totally taken off guard when everyone in the room began looking to me to lead which was completely unexpected. My first thought was, you guessed it, "I can't do this; we need one of those Bible majors in here to do this," but the arrow continued to point to me. So I said *yes* and took the bull by the horns. I went for it and led a prayer session over the next hour or so which I had never done before. Leadership was never something I sought after, but it found a way to find me!

My leadership story for the next few years continued with one word: *yes!* I decided I would simply say yes to whatever opportunities I felt God was presenting to me. These included substitute teaching, coaching, serving as a special education teacher, teaching night school and a college class, writing a grant and leading a Native American summer school program, launching a new alternative high school from scratch, starting a Christian coffee house, planting a church and commuting forty-five miles each way to get my MA degree. One thing just led to another as I said *yes* to God again and again.

Everything that has happened in my life has been because I kept saying *yes* to what I couldn't do! Sounds crazy but it's still true to this day as I now lead the Global 4/14 Window Movement with my wife Becky. I keep telling God what I can and cannot do, but He doesn't seem to listen. What I do know is this. You will never lose when you say *yes* to God. Never!

As time passed, I began getting invited into more and more leadership situations. Since those small beginnings of my early twenties, I have personally planted two churches and raised up thirty-five pastors to launch new churches or take over existing ones. I have also led pastor conferences in many countries and had various leadership roles in the Vineyard movement, including overseeing pastors and churches. And all of this from a kid born via adultery, who went to 10 elementary school's, lived with 4 different families in my teen years, and had no future in sight. But God ... had a plan for me.

I love that phrase, "But God ..." Your life may be this or that, "But God ..." God makes all the difference in your life and ultimately determines the outcome if you dare to say *yes* to the impossible. Remember, God always calls you to do what you can't do, but what he can do through you.

SMALL BEGINNINGS

If you reflect long enough, I bet you can identify those times in your own life when you recognized God's hand, and He was calling you into leadership of some sort. Maybe like me, it started like a small mustard seed but over time grew into something bigger. (I know it's cliché but, seriously, don't despise the season of small beginnings in your life.) My time in Tehachapi—a community of just four thousand people—was so instrumental in God's preparing me for what was to come. This included being bi-vocational and leading our small church which, on its best day, had around sixty attendees (including kids, unborn children, and anything that moved we counted). Who would have known that years later, I would be leading a church of over two thousand with multiple staff members, multiple church plants, and speaking at pastoral seminars and conferences around the globe? What I learned in leading our tiny church in Tehachapi has been fundamental to my leadership style and values that has carried over to this day. All this was from small beginnings that sprouted into something more as time went on.

PETER WALKS ON WATER

I love the story of Peter out on the Sea of Galilee and the disciples were terrified when they saw Jesus walking on the water. Then Jesus said, *"Take courage! it is I. Don't be afraid"* (Matt. 14:27 NIV). At this encounter, Peter blurted out, *"If it's really you, tell me to come to you, walking on the water"* (Matt. 14:28 NLT). Peter must have been thinking that there was no way he would get an answer from God. Then the next thing he heard is "Come" and—bam—he jumped out of the boat and started walking on the water toward Jesus. What was he thinking?

I can picture the disciples saying, "Peter stop, what are you doing, are you crazy? You can't walk on water; get back here in the boat with us." But he kept going until the wind picked up and he began to sink, needing rescue by lifeguard Jesus who put him back in the boat. I doubt that the other disciples chided him with, "Peter, what were you thinking? You started okay, but you took your eyes off Jesus and sank." More likely, their reaction would have been, "Peter, what was it like? You did it! You actually walked on the water." I don't think they would have focused on the sinking but on the walking!

For me, I would rather walk on water for two minutes and sink than live my whole life on a boat wondering what it's like to come to Jesus on the water. The key for Peter here was not to take a risk for risk's sake, but when he heard Jesus say "come," he had to go. Sometimes we talk ourselves out of obeying God. When we hear him say "come," it's time to go.

HEMORRHOIDS IN MENNONITE COUNTRY

I traveled to Marion, Kansas, to conduct my first solo healing and equipping conference for about three hundred people in a very conservative Mennonite Church group. The people there were longing to experience more of the Holy Spirit and spiritual gifts—and I was excited about the opportunity to share with them. During the conference, things were progressing really well when I felt it was time to take a risk and see what God would do.

In our final session, I spoke about hearing God and how we can receive words of knowledge from the Lord. This included things like sometimes it comes as a thought, a specific word, an impression, or a pain in our body that wasn't there before. So, I prayed and waited for quite a while before asking, "Is anybody getting anything that you think just might be from the Lord?" Finally, way in the back row, a woman raised her hands and said she had the word "hemorrhoids" come to her mind. I said, "That is great, so who here has the hemorrhoids?" Not surprisingly, no one responded. I followed up by saying, "It's okay if she is wrong, but this woman took a huge step of faith here tonight so if you have this condition, please let us know." At that moment, a man in the front row on the right side sheepishly raised his hand. I was elated and excited to move on to the next step.

Now I had predetermined that the person who got the word would be the person who would come and pray for the person with the condition. So in front of 300 conservative Mennonite church people, I said to the woman who had the word, "I want you to come down here and lay your hands on his hemorrhoids and ask God to heal him." With a look of horror she balked and waved me off with her hands, explaining that she wasn't going to do that.

I said, "No worries, I will help you." At that point, the man up front was ready to run out of the room. (Yes, this actually happened.)

Teri Powell, who was on our ministry team, finally came up and whispered in my ear, "You don't know what hemorrhoids are, do you?"

"Isn't that a sinus condition?" I asked. She said *no* and proceeded to tell me—to my horror—what it was.

At that moment, I considered just how much I wanted to die—or at least disappear. I was mortified what I'd done to these very conservative people who were stepping out for the first time into the supernatural. I had nowhere to run, so I admitted to the group that I didn't know what hemorrhoids were and they exploded with laughter which completely broke the ice in the room. Crazily enough, the man who was in severe pain at the time came up to me and told me that all his pain was gone. That sparked faith in the room as many now began sharing words they got and God began to heal people all over the room. It was incredible.

In the aftermath, I had this picture that God was up in heaven and motioned to Michael the archangel to come over saying, "Watch this. Rick is doing a healing conference for the first time, but he doesn't know what hemorrhoids are. This should be fun!" I can attest to the fact that it was not at all fun on my end, but it turned out to be a great lesson later on. Even though I felt foolish, by saying *yes* to the Lord, many people experienced healing and they also prayed for others for the first time. I didn't really know what I was doing, but God knew what He wanted to do. I look back and think He was pleased that I said *yes* that day and took a risk. I concluded that being a fool for Christ might not be so bad after all. Trusting God for the impossible is not a one-time event but a lifestyle to be lived. I wonder if heaven doesn't have a lot of laughter watching us.

By the way, trusting God is not just a young person's game—it's for all of us at every age. When we dare to trust God for what seems impossible, life continues to be the adventure it was meant to be! OGs, hear me on this: You may be retired from your job, but there is no retirement from Gods' kingdom adventure! And for every young leader reading this, consider this the call to your off-road journey.

God has a huge track record in using people who feel they can't do something, but they end up saying *yes* and doing it anyway. Joshua, Moses, Jeremiah, David, Paul, *you*? They each looked at themselves and said, "No way." But in the end, they said *yes* and the rest is history, just as it can be for you. Jesus told a great parable about this in Matthew 21:29-31. It's about two sons when one says, "No, I won't go," but later changed his mind and went. The other son says, "Yes, sir, I will," but he didn't go. At the end of the day, *yes* is not just what you say but what you actually do. **Good intentions change nothing, but saying and doing** *yes* **changes everything.**

Again, God never asks if you *can* **do something—he only**

asks if you *will*. This is the place where miracles are born, where we step beyond what we can do into what only God can do! So you say, "I haven't done this before." Guess what? There is a first time for everything. Your bottom line is not **"can you,"** but **"will you?"** Our string of *yeses* is like building a bridge from where we are to cross a chasm to where God has called us to go. And it pleases God so much when we give Him our *yes*.

SAYING YES TO THE OFF-ROAD JOURNEY

Going off road means saying *yes* to the unconventional, the unthinkable, the impossible, improbable, and the road less traveled. Everything that God has done in my life has been about saying *yes* to what is in front of me, starting with Jesus in 1970.

Sometimes we hesitate saying *yes* because we look at ourselves and say, "There is no way. I can't do this!" When you look at the characters of the Bible, you quickly realize that God always calls people to do what they did not feel capable of doing.

Why would God call you to do what you can't do? To stretch you and teach you to depend on Him for all you do. It's about what can happen in a life surrendered to Him. When you say *yes* to what seems impossible in your life, you are opening the door for God's miracles. If you only say *yes* to what you think you can do, you will not go very far in life or ministry. Going off road means not playing it safe. It so pleases God when you step out in faith and trust Him: *"And it is impossible to please God without faith. Anyone who wants to come to him must believe that God exists and that he rewards those who who sincerely seek him"* (Heb. 11:6 NLT). I love what my mentor John Wimber said, "Faith is spelled R-I-S-K." I think we could also spell it T-R-Y!

For a large chunk of my life I have felt the challenge of constantly being in over my head. Over and over again, I told God that I can't do this or that, find someone else, but I could not get God to back off! Kind of like Moses saying, "Here am I, send Aaron!"

Then I realized that this sounded like everyone else in the Bible whom God called. God continually called people to do what they could not see themselves doing.

Have you figured out yet that saying "I can't do this" never flies with God? When God called Gideon to fight the Midianites, "Are you kidding? I can't do this! God, you don't understand who I am. I am the low one on the totem pole." The Lord then tells Gideon that he is indeed going and he will strike down the Midianites. After some heavy negotiating like we tend to do with God, Gideon took a risk and did what the Lord asked him to do and was part of a great victory. But the victory came only because Gideon dared to say *yes* to what seemed impossible. (Read Judges 6-7.)

As recorded in Exodus 3, after forty years in the "woodshed" of Midian, Moses was tending the sheep of his father-in-law Jethro when God called to Moses from a burning bush. (I think that when you hear a voice coming out of a burning bush, it's best to give it a listen.) God told Moses that He chose Moses to be the deliverer of Israel from the oppression of their Egyptian taskmasters. Moses' response? "Are you kidding? I am eighty years old. I can't do that." After offering excuse after excuse, Moses ended up going to Pharaoh and declaring, "Thus says the Lord, Let my people go." Results were mixed at first as things got worse before they got better. (Saying *yes* does not always mean everything goes well.)

You can read the entire story in Exodus, chapters 3-14, but I'll summarize what happened. After all the plagues were over and they were on their way out of Egypt, Moses raised his staff and the Red Sea opened up and they walked through it on dry land. It was a miracle of God for sure, but it was Moses' *yes* that activated it all. Moses said *yes* to one impossibility after the other. There was no warm-up, no training ground. He was now in the Major League, having never done anything like this before. But God had something more if only Moses would dare to believe and say *yes*. It's the same dynamic that God has with you too. When God challenges you to do something, all He wants is for you to just say *yes*.

THE RIPPLE EFFECT OF YES

Your *yes* can launch a multitude of *yeses* from those you love and serve. The first ripple effect of *yes* might be your family, which can open the door to your family discovering a life and future with Jesus. My stepfather, grandmother, and two uncles, who were all far away from God, ended up coming to Christ as a result of my first *yes* to God. Your *yes* may be the first in your family line, but watch how the ripple effect works in them. My *yes* to Tehachapi opened the door to many saying *yes* to God as well—and then in Colorado, thousands more came to Christ and many churches were launched as well. Think of the ripple effect in terms of how the apostles Paul, Peter, or the early church fathers launched the church.

THE COURAGE TO SAY NO!

Sometimes it may actually take more courage to say *no* to those golden opportunities rather than saying *yes*. Your *no* to one thing may actually open up a new door to something even better. Perhaps you might be afraid of disappointing people or seeing an opportunity pass you by. Saying *no* to the good allows you to say *yes* to the great! Either way, refuse to allow fear to guide your decisions. It's not about just saying *yes* to everything that comes your way but being particular and discerning as you explore possibilities that present themselves. When you look at those who have accomplished amazing things, you will also discover that somewhere along the way they had to say *no* to good things that would take them in the wrong direction.

Mordecai Ham

Most people have heard of the name "Billy Graham," but very few have ever heard of Mordecai Ham and his ripple effect of his *yes* to God and to preaching the gospel in the 1930s. Born in 1877, he resisted God's call to become an evangelist because he wanted to be a salesman. His father and grandfather were both preachers, who both had lived in poverty. And Mordecai did not want that kind of life. Eventually he said *yes* and answered God's call on his life to preach. In one of his meetings, a sixteen-year-old farm boy wandered in and ended up giving his life to Jesus Christ that day. Billy Graham, that sixteen-year-old teenager, also said *yes* to preach the gospel as well and led more people to Christ than anyone in history. Thanks to the ripple effect of *yes*, millions of people followed Jesus for the first time.

Nam Soo Kim

Luis Bush in his book, *The Yes Effect*, shared the powerful story of Nam Soo Kim, a very influential and accomplished pastor in Queens. Growing up in a Buddhist family in South Korea, Nam Soo Kim had a life-changing encounter with Jesus. Having survived serving in the military and then dealing with multiple failures in the business world, he found none of the peace that Buddhism promised. At the lowest place in his life, he considered suicide. With nowhere else to turn, he wandered into the evening service of a local church where the presence of God overwhelmed him, convincing him of God's existence. He also believed that God had a purpose for keeping him alive. At first, his family sneered at his new-found faith and thought he'd lost his mind. To the contrary, his *yes* to God, and his brother's later miraculous healing from leukemia, opened the door for his family to leave Buddhism and embrace Jesus. Nam Soo Kim's personal faith had started a chain reaction that could not be stopped.

But it was just the beginning. He and his wife then started a church in the slums of Seoul, and years later, he ended up in New York City where he planted Promise Church, which was fitting as he had made God a promise to follow Him anywhere and do what He said to do. That church has grown to thousands today, influencing hundreds of thousands more worldwide. He also has helped launch—along with Wess Stafford, Luis Bush, and Bob Hoskins—a new global movement called the 4/14 Window Movement, which my wife Becky and I now have the privilege of leading.

Nam Soo Kim's *yes* has opened the door for Becky and me to say *yes* as well—and now thousands more are saying *yes* to raising up a generation to change the world.

Becky's Story of Yes!

When I was younger, I never thought of myself as someone who could hear God's voice. It has been an ongoing process of learning to discern the thoughts that come into my mind. "Is that just me? Could it be God?" And they always seem to come when I least expect to hear from Him.

One Saturday morning, I was attending a training workshop Rick was teaching at our church. My only purpose in being there was to support him. Toward the end of the morning, while I was sitting in the back of the room, not really listening, God popped a question into my mind:

"What if you just say* yes *to everything that comes your way regarding kids?"

I took a moment to think about what that could mean. I had no idea what it would look like, but I felt like there was some kind of adventure ahead for me if I would dare to trust God and say yes. I thought about a surfer riding a wave in the ocean. The surfer was at the will of the wave to go where it would take her or him.

I decided, "I can do that!" That seemed simple enough. Well, little did I know where my yes *would take me.*

In just a couple of months, my yes took me to attend a one-day conference on child hunger. Next, I was asked to come and consult a church on the strengths and weaknesses of their kids program. Then I got an email inviting me to attend a conference on holistic child development in the local church in <u>Singapore</u>! I was about to delete the email. I don't go to conferences in exotic places. But then I caught myself. Could this all be part of saying yes *to everything that comes my way regarding kids?*

After sharing with Rick what I thought God had said to me, he affirmed that I needed to go and follow through with my commitment to say yes. *We both ended up going and the conference was unbelievable! One thousand people representing ninety two nations, all passionate about God's heart for children. These were my people!!*

It changed my life in ways I couldn't have ever imagined before being there. Not only was I changed, but Rick's heart was ignited, too, while in Singapore. We were forever committed to joining with what God is doing with kids and youth. An opportunity to say yes, *one after another, just continued to happen. It eventually led us to starting a nonprofit called Generation Now, which is based on the values we saw demonstrated at the conference, and we were later asked to lead the 4/14 Movement (another* yes*), the organization that put on the Singapore conference. This yes to His adventure for my life positioned me for living a life with passion and purpose.*

When we were pastoring our church in Fort Collins, every once in a while, I would be asked to give the talk (often referred to as a sermon) on Sunday morning. Because it wasn't something I did all the time, it was really important to me that what I shared was delivered well and connected with the people who were listening.

On this particular Sunday, after the first of two services, I felt like I had struggled with my talk. As I stepped off the stage and listened to the music, I decided to ask God how He thought I did. In my heart I whispered, "God, how do you think I did presenting the message I felt You had given me for the day?" I waited quietly for his response. I honestly wanted to hear His opinion.

After a few moments of silence, I responded back to God, "Really, you have nothing to say?" Then I heard that familiar, quiet voice in my heart, "Becky, I don't even think like you do. When you were asked to teach, and you said yes, I was pleased. It doesn't even matter how you did speaking today. When you said yes, you made yourself available for Me to work through you. My ability to work in people's hearts isn't dependent on how well you do; it's about My power and what I can do."

Becky Olmstead, Vineyard USA kids director
Global 4/14 Movement co-leader

What about you? Is God asking you to step out in faith and follow Him in some adventure? The adventure begins with your *yes*! You never know where one *yes* could lead you. Each day we have opportunities to be a part of what He is doing around us. The risky part is saying *yes* before you know what you'll be asked to do; it is a very real step of faith. Does God have your *yes*? God is looking for a generation of people who are willing to do just that. You can take that step because God always has your back. Ask God to order your day and keep your eyes open for opportunities to say *yes*.

QUESTIONS OF THE HEART

1. Can you remember times when you said *yes* to God beyond your capabilities? What happened?

2. What is the ripple effect of someone's *yes* in your life?

3. How has your *yes* impacted someone else? What about your *no*?

4. What do you need to say *yes* to right now?

5. Do you remember a time when saying *no* to something opened up a greater door of opportunity?

6. Can you recall missed opportunities because you were afraid to say *yes*?

7. What would it take for you to say *yes* to the off-road journey?

EIGHT
USE IT OR LOSE IT: THE FUTILITY OF POTENTIAL

I loved coaching various high school sports before entering full-time ministry. As a coach, athletes with great potential used to impress me. There were some who were incredibly big, strong, fast, and very athletic. Some of them turned out to be pretty good, but many never stepped up to the plate to fully develop their natural talent. Sadly, they ended up with their "potential" intact. I had many on our teams who surpassed those more naturally talented athletes because they worked their tails off and improved day after day.

That underscored an important truth for me: It's not about using what you wish you had, but using what you do have! I remember Jim Abbot who became a top MLB pitcher and Olympic medalist—all while having only one hand. Abbott was born with a physical disability, as he had a deformed right arm. As a kid playing baseball, he was told over and over that he would not be able to keep up with the competition. He did not give up and eventually had a successful pitching career at the University of Michigan and with the Los Angeles Angels in the Major Leagues. Abbott impressed audiences with his ability to catch the ball, remove his glove, and quickly throw the ball again, all while using just one hand. It was something special to see. He used what he had, not what he wished he had, and he had to go off road and against the grain to fulfill his dreams.

When I saw one player—let's call him Dan—at our first practice, I thought that we had something really special and he could carry our team to new heights. He was heads above all the rest from day one. The challenge was convincing Dan he needed to work to get better, something I did not succeed in doing. And by the end of the season, he was just another pretty good football player, though he had the potential to be really great.

Like most teams, our football team hated wind sprints just like I did when I played in high school. To the casual bystander, our players looked like they were exhausted and regularly whined that they couldn't do anymore. But I knew there was more in them, so I pushed them against their natural inclination, beyond what they believed was their limit. I did not want to kill them, but I knew they had more potential than they thought they had. My players didn't appreciate this at the time, but they sure did in the fourth quarter when they had something left because of those wind sprints. Sometimes we need people to help us push through past barriers to the potential that we can't see in ourselves.

I am no longer impressed with potential—not with staff, ministry, leadership, myself, or even churches. Resumes are just a glimpse of people's past and future potential, but there are no guarantees of success. You are not supposed to die with your potential, but many do. I think the worst headstone anyone could ever have is, "He/She had so much potential." How awful, a life wasted, rather than a life lived to the fullest!

SO MUCH POTENTIAL

Potential can mean you're talented in a particular area, but I'll take the hard worker over the more talented any day. In sports, we see this dynamic played out all the time. For example, the NBA championship team wins a title because of its chemistry, hard

USE IT OR LOSE IT: THE FUTILITY OF POTENTIAL

work and execution, not because of the players' collective potential.

When we see an athlete, a musician, a dancer, a singer, a student, or any number of people within a profession, we often say, "That person has so much potential." How many people do you know who have incredible or extraordinary talents and gifts but never used them? Many with less natural talent can actually end up going much further because they use what they have, which is a principle of the kingdom. If you use what God has given to you, you get more. If you don't, even what you have goes away. We are stewards, not owners. God has made an investment in you and me—and He wants a return on His investment. Leave your potential behind and go for the kingdom with what you have.

I experienced this when Becky and I went to Colorado to start a church from scratch with no money and no team. *What were we thinking? Quitting the best jobs of our lives and moving to Colorado? What if we were wrong?* At one point in our process, the fear of failure became less than the potential fear of regret. What if this really is what God is asking us to do? The bigger risk was looking back at the end of our lives (like now) and wondering if that had been God's design for us or not. The only way to find out was to take the step and go big, so we did and the rest is history.

Some of you might have already realized that God is not an equal opportunity gift giver. He gives more to some than to others—but everyone gets something! What matters most is not what He has given to someone else but what He has given to us!

Crazily, in God's kingdom if you use whatever you have, it grows to even more. Rather than moan about what you don't have and what others have (I have done plenty of that), saying, "God, why did you give so much to her or him?" Thank Him for what He has given you, use it, and watch it grow.

In Matthew 25:14-29, Jesus, the great storyteller, shares powerful principles known as the parable of the Bags of

Silver. Though its context is about money, the principles are very relevant to our discussion here.

In this story, a wealthy landowner was going on a long trip and called together his servants to entrust them with various amounts of his money while he was gone. To one he gave five bags of silver, to another he gave two and to a third he gave just one, all in proportion to their abilities. Interesting that he did not give each one three and see how they did. He knew how much they could handle and gave accordingly. So it works with us. God gives us what He knows we can handle, and it's important to not compare ourselves to what others have.

On his return, the landowner gathered them together again so they could give an account of how they did with the owner's money. The one who had been given five invested it and ended up with ten. The servant with two also doubled what he had and now had four. But the servant with just one had an attitude about how little was given to him and refused to do anything with it. He gave the bag back to the owner. The master was full of praise to the first two and gave them both a big, "Well done, good and faithful servant!" But there were no praises or "well done" affirmations given to the third servant who made excuses and played the blame game. **As long as you have someone to blame for what you are or what you're not, you have no way forward**. The owner then called this servant out. He said, "You wicked and lazy servant" (Matt. 25:26 NLT). Wow, wicked? When we do not use what God gives to us, He calls it wicked. Think about that. Jesus says it is a *wicked* thing to waste what God has entrusted to you.

Then in the next moment, the master/owner took the one bag from this servant and gave it to the one who had ten. Something inside me objects, thinking, "Why would you give more to the one who has the most? Why not give the one to the servant who had four to equal things out?"

Then Jesus gave the punch line: "To those who use what they have been given, even more will be given, and they will have an abundance. But from those who do nothing with what they have, [here it comes] even that will be taken away from them" (Matt. 25:29 NLT).

What can we learn from this parable/story?

1. Using or not using what God has given you is a BIG deal. If you use what God has given to you, you get more! And one day, we will give an account of what we did or didn't do with what He gave us.

2. You always get enough to start. The "someday," and "if I only had more" attitude is self-deception and leads to nowhere.

3. Good intentions change nothing ... but taking action changes everything. Hearer or doer? Sand or solid ground? What are you saying *no* to simply because of a lack of resources or how you see yourself? What is that thing that gnaws at you that never goes away? What is that knot in your stomach, that ache in your heart?

4. It's up to God to decide what you get, but it's up to you whether you use it or lose it.

You might start out as a one-talent person but end up as a ten- or twenty-bag of silver person because you used what God gave you. I might have been one of those one-bag people when I started, which I wasn't always happy about. But that's not true anymore because I used what I had, which did not seem like much at the time, but it has grown exponentially over the years. I wish I was a six-foot-four, two hundred-thirty pound fast and strong star athlete in high school. Turns out I was six inches shorter and eighty pounds lighter, and equipped with a slow, weak, and an average-athletic body. (I can't believe I just admitted this.) *Come on, God, what is up with this?* When I reflect on this now, I can see that God made me and gave me just what I needed for what He has called me to do. And the same goes for you!

WHAT'S HOLDING YOU BACK?

Whether you are born with a talent for something or you have a skill that you've developed through education, training, and life experience, these potentials are completely meaningless and useless if you don't do something with them. Walking around in life with a handful of academic degrees might impress some people, but without applying that knowledge in some way, it's useless.

Do you think Tiger Woods would've been successful had he not put in countless hours practicing and training? It's quite possible that he had a natural knack for golf from birth, but without developing those skills, he wouldn't be much better than the weekend warrior at your local municipal golf course.

Maybe you are one of those who are uncomfortable with getting outside of your comfort zone. Or, like some who may fear success, you unwittingly sabotage your chances of achieving it. Your full potential isn't a destination; it's a path. It's a freedom journey, an adventure where you go beyond your own limitations and the limitations that others (even with good intentions) put upon you. The Bible describes God as being "able to do exceedingly abundantly above all that we ask or think" (Ephesians 3:20 American Standard Version), and tells us that with Him "nothing will be impossible" (Luke 1:37 ESV). He is always able to do far more than we could even think of asking Him.

If you are going to reach your potential, it is imperative that you have an ongoing relationship with God, one where you keep on connecting with Him and growing in your faith. There is not a person alive today who has not been gifted by God. No one but God knows the potential inside you, that untapped power, dormant ability, and unused strength you uniquely possess. It is time to start thinking bigger thoughts, praying bigger prayers, believing God has more for you than what you're currently experiencing. It is time to surrender fully to Him, exercise your faith, realize your potential, and go for it! Fear not, for the Lord your God is with you! (Isaiah 41:10)

QUESTIONS FOR THE HEART

1. What gifts and talents do you have?

2. Are you using them? Why or why not?

3. Are you living up to your potential?

4. What do you need to do to get started?

5. Do you have a problem comparing yourself to others?

6. What is holding you back from taking a risk?

7. What would you do if you had no fear?

NINE
REFUSE SAUL'S ARMOR

DAVID WENT off road when he refused to wear Saul's armor to fight Goliath. Everybody loves the story of David slaying the giant Goliath with his slingshot, but my favorite part is actually the preparation before the main event! As the story in 1 Samuel 17 goes, no one was willing to fight the giant and then young David raises his hand and says, "What's the problem here? Nobody wants to take this guy out? Sign me up; I am ready to go. Somebody has to do this, so it might as well be me." I'm not sure if they laughed or not, but since no one else volunteered, what harm was there in letting him try? To get him ready, they took him into Saul's armory to fit him for battle. David, as a shepherd boy apparently had no armor of his own, so Saul's would have to suffice. One small problem was that Saul was a man of huge stature, and his armor worked well for him—but not for David.

I love what David did next. "Hey guys, I appreciate all this, but this doesn't work for me. I can barely move." David must have looked pretty silly in that armor. "Yeah, I know this is what you all do and it works for you, but I can't do this."

Does that sound like an off-road moment? I can hear David saying, "If I am going to fight this giant, I need to do it my way. Actually, I am pretty good with a sling shot, so let's go with that."

So he went and faced off against the giant Goliath and triumphed to become one of the greatest underdog stories in all of human history. God used David "just being David" to bring victory for Israel over the giant.

Those who had tried to put the armor on David probably had great intentions. This armor was tried and tested in battle for years. And it was what they knew and thought David needed to succeed, but it wasn't who David was. Incredibly, he had the grit to refuse it. Maybe it took as much courage for David to say no to these powerful people (can you imagine the pressure?) as it did for him to face the giant Goliath. For David, it became an up-or-down deal. Win or lose, this is the way it's going to be. But let's be clear: David's trust was never in the armor or the slingshot; rather, it was always in the power of the living God. It's pretty incredible how he displayed courage to not only face the giant Goliath but also to stand up for himself in crunch time. He wasn't being rebellious. He was just being honest with them.

It is important to note that there appears to be no rebellion in David's heart, which is often mistakenly attributed to those who go "off road" or against the grain. David had an attitude of honor. He essentially told Saul, "I know this is the way it's always done and the way I am supposed to do it and I don't want to dishonor you, but I can't do it your way." And God honored the young man as he swam against the current, against the majority opinion, against conventional thought. What a powerful lesson for young leaders going off road today.

SAUL'S ARMOR DIDN'T FIT DAVID (AND IT WON'T FIT YOU)

The story offers us great principles for going off road today. For young leaders, it's a real deal when you face the pressure to fall in line with insecure leaders (and parents) who want you to be like them and follow their dreams for your life. It would have been quite sad if David had said, "I appreciate the help, but I can't do this so I am going to take my little slingshot and head home. I can never be like Saul." A big takeaway from this story is that **you only have grace to be you and nobody else!** When you try to be somebody you're not, you look foolish and end up on your own—and that's no fun, trust me.

Some well-meaning people may try—or already have tried—to conform you to their image of what they think your life should be. One of the biggest challenges you might face is the pressure of living out the expectations of others, including teachers, parents, and leaders. Everybody seems to have a plan for your life. Have you ever noticed that? And not everyone will be excited about your off-road journey!

What do Elvis Presley, Shohei Ohtani, Dua Lipa, and Dwayne Johnson have in common? They all had people trying to make them something they weren't—as they struggled to go against the grain to follow their dreams.

Elvis Presley

After a performance at Nashville's Grand Ole Opry, Elvis Presley was told by the concert hall manager that he was better off returning to Memphis and driving trucks, which was his former career. Aren't we all glad he refused to put on Saul's armor and become a truck driver?

Shohei Ohtani

As a Japanese professional baseball pitcher, designated hitter, and outfielder for the Los Angeles Angels, Shohei Ohtani dared to forge a new path foreign to the modern sport. All the doomsayers said that a two-way player could not make it in the Majors. He proved them wrong by being the first player since Babe Ruth to be selected to the MLB All Star Game as a pitcher *and* a position player. He refused to wear Saul's armor and went off road, and he's making history today because of it.

Dwayne Johnson

Born to a Canadian professional wrestler, Dwayne Johnson very much grew up surrounded by the sport of wrestling. In his early life, Dwayne took to football and played with the Calgary Stampeders—but not for long. He was cut from the team during his first season. Dwayne decided to take after his father and grandfather and pursue wrestling. His dad pushed back against his son's new career interest and told him not to do it. Little did Rocky Johnson know that his son would go on to become one of the World Wrestling Entertainment's most successful wrestlers, leading him to his first feature film role in *The Mummy Returns*.

Dua Lipa

Dua Lipa is a British singer/songwriter with hit single after single. Interestingly, when she was 11 years old, she was told she couldn't sing. Eager to show her talent, she joined a choir but was told she didn't fit the choir because her voice was too low. If they could only see her now at 30 years old as she is reportedly worth around $16 million with millions of albums sold!

OF COURSE, parents have dreams for their children and rightfully so. But sometimes they put pressure on them to be what they were not able to be themselves. A parent may want or need their kids to follow in their footsteps to feel better about themselves. Many well-meaning parents have a plan for their kids to follow but are devastated when they choose a different path.

The much quoted Bible verse in Proverbs 22:6 has often been misconstrued: "Start children off on the way they should go, and even when they are old they will not turn from it" (NIV). Scripture clearly says, "on the way **they** should go," not "the way *you* want them to go." I have heard many times—and used to believe —that kids are a blank slate for us to write on. Now I totally disagree with that statement. Rather than a blank slate, I believe they are actually more like a book to be read. Who are they? What are their gifts and talents? How are they wired? Maybe the best parenting skill is to discover what God has put in your child and then come alongside them and help make that happen. This is what I tried to do with my two sons and also for a new generation of young leaders. You are not a blank slate either, but a book to be read by those who are willing to take the time to discover who you are and what God has put in you. And there are many more chapters of your life that continue to be written.

BEWARE OF "DRIVE-BY GUILTINGS"

My friend Larry Osborne, teaching pastor of North Coast Church in Vista, California, coined the phrase "Drive-by Guiltings," which is so descriptive of what many of us have experienced. Beware of those subtle and not so subtle whispers or shouts that come your way. They can actually be a drive-by guiltings, comments and criticisms that come from both well-meaning and not-so-well-meaning people in your life. When somebody gives you a "word from the Lord," it's important to test it by Scripture and also by those who have spiritual authority in your life.

I had one of those drive-by guiltings after my very first conference level teaching opportunity. A woman came up to me and said, "The Lord wants you to know that you have a weak anointing and you are working on yesterday's bread." Then she walked off and left me standing there as I was wondering what had just happened. That was it, not even a "... and God wants you to..." Nothing. A pure drive-by was in progress. I was jolted. It was my first time speaking at an event like that, and she had her agenda for me in that moment. The more I thought about it, for sure it was a weak anointing but it was all the "anointing" I had that night. And "yesterday's bread"? It was more like the last month's or year's bread. I pulled everything I knew into it.

Though there was some truth in what she shared, there was no love within a mile of it and she gave me no encouragement or sense of what I should do.

God doesn't do that to us. If that was indeed a word from the Lord, there would have been something like, "Rick I want you to prepare and study more," or "I want you to seek My face more next time." Something, anything. God doesn't perform "drive-by guiltings," but sadly, His followers sometimes do.

In this case, I went to some of those who had spiritual authority in my life and shared the "word" given to me. Each said they felt it was clearly not from the Lord and prayed for me to not get slimed (which I did) by what I heard. They also challenged me to never again receive a personal word/prophecy from someone without having someone else whom I knew present for protection and accountability. I have tenaciously followed this advice for the last forty years and encourage you to do it as well. But at the same time, it's so important to ask God, "Is there any part of this that *is* for me?"

Don't let these drive-bys derail you or discourage you from listening to all prophetic type words that come your way. You need to have some safeguards in place for sure, but stay humble and open to hearing what God might have to say through those He brings into your life. I have found that when God typically speaks to me in this way, it usually confirms something I have been dealing with rather than something out of left field. Paul told the Corinthians that "prophecy/words from the Lord" were given to strengthen, encourage, and to bring comfort. (1 Cor. 14:3) When you receive a "word" from someone that does not fit this description, you need to suspect its authenticity. Furthermore, Paul, not wanting us to reject prophecy altogether, tells us in 1 Thessalonians 5:20-22, "Do not treat prophecies with contempt but test them all; hold on to what is good, reject every kind of evil" (NIV).

I remember in my earliest days of ministry somebody came up to me and announced, "You are no Chuck Smith." (I was part of the Calvary Chapel movement led by Pastor Chuck, who was also an iconic leader and Bible teacher of the Jesus Movement.) This threw me for a loop as I didn't think I was trying to be like Chuck Smith, though his influence was certainly evident in my teaching. At least I didn't think I was? Looking back, I thought, "Come on, I was just twenty-five years old and Pastor Chuck was a seasoned teacher and a leader of a movement." I felt a curse was placed around my neck and wondered how I would ever measure up. Being me was not good enough; I got the message loud and clear. The reality was that Chuck Smith's armor did not fit me, though others tried to make it fit. Though I learned so much from Pastor Chuck who ordained me, I needed to figure out my own way and my own style.

Paul told Timothy in 1 Timothy 4:12 to not let people look down on him because he was young. That goes for you too. You can't be who you aren't yet or who you will be in the future. You can't be a mature 50-year-old leader when you are 23! I sure wasn't. But you can be the best 23-year-old you can be! Use your slingshot—or whatever God has gifted you with—and go make a difference and change the world.

Diane Leman, a friend of mine, shares an off-road story of how she had to reject Saul's armor to be the leader God called her to be. She was told over and over again what she could not do simply because she was a woman. Here is Diane's story in her own words!

Diane's Story

To young women leaders...

Women be silent! Women cover your heads. Women serve the coffee. Women stay home. Women submit to men. Women must not teach. Women do not study. Women do not lead! Such were the mantras of the faith in which I was raised. Here the roles of men and women were clearly defined, not only by the church doctrine but purportedly by God Himself in His Word. While not all Christian communities adhere to these specific rules, there are still a vast number of Christian institutions and organizations that forbid women to preach, teach, and lead. The controversy continues well into the twenty-first century as documented by the constant flurry of books, podcasts and blog posts that contend for each side. Younger women leaders, like many of you, have enjoyed greater freedom. However, many will still encounter plenty of hostility and hindrances as they seek to live out their God-given calling to teach, preach and lead. Yes! YOUR GOD-GIVEN CALLING! This is what changed everything for me. As a young woman, I struggled with the burning desire I had to communicate God's truth and love with my own voice, a woman's voice. I loved being on my high school debate team. I was energized by my brief foray into theater, and I excelled in my speech classes at the University of Illinois. I proudly taught in public education for six years. I searched the Scriptures to satisfy my hunger to know Jesus better and be ready to share Him boldly with others. However, I was forbidden to even give out a hymn number for group singing in our Sunday assembly! Because I wanted to please God and obey Him, I acquiesced to the rules, suffocated my true personality and gifts, and suffered in silence. Literally!

Then came an amazing encounter with the Holy Spirit who I had rarely even heard about. But suddenly, I experienced being filled with His very Presence. And just like the day of Pentecost, I awakened to God's heart for women, Acts 2:17:

> *"And in the last days it shall be, God declares that I will pour out my Spirit on all flesh, and your sons and your daughters shall prophesy," (ESV).*

God's call is not about gender. He pours out His Spirit on all, including women. Jesus alone decides who you are and what you can do! My eyes were opened to the love and respect and empowerment Jesus had for women in the Gospels and continues to have today. I said yes to Him over 45 years ago, and I have not stopped contending for all women to know the love of Jesus, the empowering of the Holy Spirit, and the freedom to embrace His call to be who He says each of us is. Has there been pushback? Yes! But I have also experienced the favor of Jesus, a wonderful supportive husband, an awesome church community, and the Vineyard USA. The world needs to hear women's voices like yours that unashamedly and openly declare, "Jesus is Lord!"

Dianne Leman, speaker, author, pastor

SAUL'S ARMOR OF MARRIAGE?

Part of Saul's armor that people try to put on you is the lie that you need to be married to be an effective leader. "*You can't be the leader you need to be until you get married.*" Ever heard something like that? I believe God wants to encourage you to live your singleness to the fullest. Do what you can uniquely do as a single person. Don't buy the lie that you have to be married to reach your full potential. Marriage will come when it comes—if it comes. Too many leaders have felt pressure to get married, and it ended up in disaster. I heard this over and over again as a young single guy: "*If you want to be successful and go to the next level, you need to get married.*" I actually did six weddings as a single pastor and led a church of mostly married folks for three years. If you're not married yet, don't waste your single life. It is a gift and a great asset for the kingdom of God. It's okay to be single...really! By the way, Jesus was single...for His whole life, and He was totally fulfilled in His life!

Personally, I struggle with the "You Complete Me" rhetoric! It makes being single second class. Paul helps us out when he says that, for some, it is better to be single. Actually, sometimes it is, and sometimes it's not! There are some things you can do because you are single, and there are other things you can do because you are married. Some people will relate to you because you are single, others because you are married. I enjoyed doing singles seminars and later did seminars on marriage (after I married Becky). While I am much better at the marriage deal after forty years of it, I did my best with what I had in those early days.

EMBRACING MARRIAGE

At the same time, it's no sin to want to be married. God cares about that and knows your desire for intimate relationships and finding a partner in life and ministry. When the time comes, embrace being married and leave the single life and mindset behind, but cutting the cord of singleness may not be so easy. Counselors sometimes say that the later you get married in life the better your chance for a good marriage. But getting married later in life also presents some challenges as you have become used to being quite independent, calling all the shots, and having everything your way.

If or when you **decide to get married, you choose a "shared life" with another person**. Are you ready to have someone around you *all the time*? Not being able to take off for the weekend with the boys or the girls anytime you want? Marriage also means giving and taking, not getting your way all the time, and deferring to another person. When I was single I did not have to consult anyone about life's decisions such as what I would do with my money, my time, or my friends. It was quite the adjustment being married and slowing that train down to come to a joint decision on things. One of the early arguments Becky and I had was that I would arbitrarily make some decision without consulting her. (Like when I was single!) I would set up meetings for us with people and tell her after the fact. That did not go over well.

In a way, it was about honoring her and giving up control. Marriage means laying down your life for each other, putting the needs of your spouse above your own, it means laying down your rights, and the big one...it's not just about you anymore! Until you are willing to do this, you are not ready to be married.

Marriage needs to be an "all in" deal for it to work, which is why keeping the door of divorce open short-circuits the whole process. It's not a 50-50 proposition, half of me and half of you. It's a 100-100 commitment—all of me and all of you. Until you are ready for that level of commitment, stay single and enjoy it.

John Borman's story

I am 66 and single. Single as in never married. Often when I meet new people, they will ask, "Married?" "Kids?" When I say no, I've never been married, it most often creates an awkward moment. I have lost track of the number of times that awkward moment has occurred. And let's face it, Christian culture and even western culture is not constructed for a single person over 25. I've been engaged twice and I was most in love with a person I was never engaged to, and when it didn't work out, I was devastated. Everything was falling into place (I was 26), I had heard God's voice and marriage was the obvious next step, and it never dawned on me that it might not work out. Well, it didn't work out. I had put off so many decisions in my early life assuming that I would get married. I didn't purchase a home for quite some time and hesitated on job opportunities along the way. At some point, I had to grapple with the possibility that it may not happen. So then what? I had to change my perspective. God is ok with my singleness. The apostle Paul recommends staying single. (1 Cor.7:8) Jesus is our ultimate example and of course was single. But we also learn early on in Genesis that "it is not good that man should be alone" (Gen. 2:18). Both sides of that coin can be true.

I have learned to not seek a wife, but to seek first His kingdom. There have been times of loneliness. Certain times of the year, such as the holidays, can be more difficult. I have such a high value around family, and I sometimes wonder what it would be like to enjoy my own kids and grandkids. But God has been good, and there have been so many meaningful experiences in my life.

I've smuggled Bibles into China, I've led college groups, home groups, played golf in Scotland, and the list goes on and on. My professional career has included being an English teacher, high school principal, district superintendent, and college professor. While I could have done those things as a married man, I was able to invest differently because I am not. I am learning to forget what lies behind and to press on to lay hold of that for which He has laid hold of me. (Phil. 3:12).

To the young leader: It is not religious to seek first His kingdom. He meant it when He added that all things shall be added to you. He'll bring the right one and you really will know. If He has plans that include being single, it will be the best adventure imaginable. Learn true intimacy regardless, and trust that He knows your heart and will always have your back.

John Borman, Former high school coach, athletic director, principal, and school district superintendant. (I'm currently teaching at Colorado Christian University.)

DISPELLING A FEW MYTHS

The idea that when you get married, the lust and sexual temptation stuff will magically disappear and you won't have to deal with that anymore is—sadly—false. Do you think the evil one is out there saying, "Well, now that they are married, we might as well leave them alone and move on?" In our sex-charged culture, you are constantly bombarded from all directions and that doesn't change with marriage. Young leader, you really do want to win this battle while you are single as much as possible and bring that freedom into your future marriage. Ephesians 6:13 comes into play here. "Therefore put on the full armor of God, so that when the day of evil comes, you may be able to stand your ground, and after you have done everything, to stand" (NIV).

Another myth is that over time you will outgrow the lust and sexual issues as you age. Oh, how I wish that was true! For me it was wishful thinking. This battle did not go away when I got married and in some ways became more intense. I still fight the good fight for moral purity to this day.

Young leader, sorry to tell you, but you will fight this battle for moral purity for the rest of your life. Keep your guard up and know that it's a worthy and winnable fight. I wish someone had told me what was coming and helped me fight the battles that were to come. You need someone like that in your life if you are going to have victory in this. When you are struggling in this area, do you have someone you can go to for help?

You have no grace (strength from God) when you're trying to be something or someone you're not! You also have no grace for yesterday, and you have no grace from God for tomorrow, but you have all the grace you need for today. Like manna from heaven that the children of Israel got every morning, grace comes the same way. In Matthew 6:34, Jesus said something really important, "So don't worry about tomorrow, for tomorrow will bring its own worries. Today's trouble is enough for today" (NIV). Don't stress and worry about being married while you are single; just be the best single you can be. And don't look back on your single life either; just be the best wife or husband you can be. You have grace to be single, and you have grace to be married but not both at the same time. Embrace the season you are in!

QUESTIONS FOR THE HEART

1. Can you recall a time when you felt pressure to be something you're not?

2. How do you handle sexual temptation as a single person? As a married person?

3. In what ways have you had to reject "Saul's armor" in your life?

4. How have you experienced a drive by guilting! Describe.

5. Are you trying to live someone else's dream for your life? Explain.

6. Are you content with your present station in life? Single? Married? Dating? Engaged? Looking?

7. What does being the best you can be look like in your current situation?

TEN
DON'T SACRIFICE YOUR LIFE (OR FAMILY) ON THE ALTAR OF MINISTRY

No matter how hard you try, ministry will never satisfy the emptiness or longing of your soul. It was never supposed to. If it was, Elijah would have been the poster child as he hit the jackpot in an amazing display of God's power during his showdown at the Carmel Corral against his nemesis King Ahab. If ministry could ever satisfy the longing of our soul, it would be there, right? You would expect the following verses to describe Elijah holding a huge Holy Spirit party to celebrate. But that's not how it went down—*at all*.

Instead, with Jezebel and Ahab still out to kill Elijah, he hits the wall and he's ready to quit. Fire from heaven, enemy destroyed, victory all around, and now under a tree ready to die? What's up with that? And surprisingly enough, it's not an uncommon feeling for many of those in leadership and ministry. Like Elijah, we all hit the wall at some point and tell God that we can't or won't do this anymore. Ever been there? If you haven't, don't worry—you will! But even when we give up on God, He never gives up on us. And so was the case with Elijah.

When most teachers unpack this story, they love to focus on the clash between Elijah and Ahab, which is certainly powerful and exciting. But these days, I'm more struck by what happened in the aftermath of this great victory.

We find Elijah lying under a large broom bush, exhausted and clearly done. He blurts out, *"I have had enough Lord. Take my life; I am no better than my ancestors"* (1 Kings 19:4). Then he lays down under a bush and falls asleep. This is the part where we want to yell, "Elijah, what are you doing here? Get a grip. Why the despair? Come on, man. You need to get it together! Let's celebrate this incredible thing God has done here. After all this, you are ready to give up and die?" This just doesn't make sense, does it—until you've experienced this feeling for yourself.

Ahab and Jezebel were still chasing after him to kill him and he had to be thinking, "Oh God, when will this ever end?" Have you ever felt like that? When I first read this I thought, "Wow! If that happened to me, I would be ready to rock and roll. Bring it on, Ahab and Jezebel! Give me your best shot—we can do this!"

But not Elijah. Totally exhausted, he's lying down under a tree when an angel of the Lord shows up to give him exactly what he needed—rest and nourishment. So he fell asleep, and the angel returned and woke him and gave him something to drink and eat. Then he went back to sleep again, but the angel woke him a second time and told him to eat and drink because the journey required more to sustain him. I imagine that Elijah wasn't expecting that news.

He probably thought, "What journey? I am not going anywhere. Are you kidding? I told you I am done." But in 1 Kings 1:8, buoyed by the rest and sustenance, Elijah agreed to give it a go as he embarked on the journey, traveling for forty days and nights to Horeb, where he was to meet with God. Upon arriving, Elijah did what so many of us do as he put out his woe-is-me story.

To paraphrase 1 Kings 1:10, Elijah said, "I am all alone and the only prophet you have left. Nobody loves you but me!"

Then came the famous exchange.

God said, "Go out and stand on the mountain in the presence of the Lord, for the Lord is about to pass by" (1 Kings 19:11

NIV). And a powerful wind came, but the Lord was not in the wind. Then an earthquake came, but the Lord was not in the quake either. And finally came a gentle whisper! And the Lord asked Elijah why he was standing there. (1 Kings 19:13)

Elijah immediately returned to his woe-is-me story. Then came the big moment when God said to Elijah, "Go back the way you came" (1 Kings 19:15 NIV). I love this because it meant that God was not done with Elijah. There was no rebuke or lecture about him wanting to die and give up on God. Turns out, God still had a purpose for Elijah to complete. I believe that the point of this story is that Elijah needed God and not some great ministry moment to sustain him. So in this new place of refreshment, God sent him back to finish what He called him to do. Only this time, Elijah got a partner (Elisha) and did not have to face his enemies alone. God knew what Elijah needed! He needed God Himself, and a friend to stand beside him. So it is with you. You need God and you need friends standing with you in the fight.

God is the ultimate source of your life, not what you do! He is the one who will sustain you through the thick and thin times you will face along the way. Jesus talked about this in John 15:4-5:

> *Remain in me, and I will remain in you. For a branch cannot produce fruit if it is severed from the vine, and you cannot be fruitful unless you remain in me. Yes, I am the vine; you are the branches. Those who remain in me, and I in them, will produce much fruit. For apart from me you can do nothing" (NLT).*

Ministry is a wonderful thing ... if you can survive it! I have talked to young leaders who are leery of going into vocational ministry because of what they see in us older leaders.

Jared's Story

My name is Jared, and I was the 23-year-old who asked Rick the question, "What would you say to yourself when you were 23 if you could?" That was an important question for me as I had become quite disillusioned by much of what I had seen from some of my leaders. When I was 21, I came home after two years of ministry training to be part of the leadership team at the church where I grew up. It was very important to me to find mentors who would help me to keep growing in both a personal relationship with God and in pastoral ministry.

I identified three different people I admired and wanted to learn from. I asked each if they would be willing to spend some time sharing their wisdom with me. Yet within a few months, each one of them had fallen out of ministry. Sin, burnout, and fighting with other leaders had taken all of them out of ministry and hurt the very people they signed up to love and serve. I felt so discouraged and disappointed. I was left asking the question: "Is anyone really following Jesus and is there anyone I can trust?'" Even deeper inside of me, a fear rose up that I would somehow end up just like them.

This sudden fear definitely rattled my ideas of what it meant to be a leader and especially a pastor. It felt like so few people (if any) were really doing ministry well. As I reflect on those circumstances, I have learned that just because a leader appears successful doesn't mean they are really living a good life underneath. I think that experience also taught me that I can't determine who is really following Jesus. All I can do is try my best to follow Jesus and lead others in the integrity of my own heart.

What I would say to other young leaders like myself is that we should take our example from people who have been faithful for a long time rather than those who do not have a proven track record. This is why I sought out someone like Rick Olmstead who has had forty years of "successful" ministry. I am sure there are some other good examples and role models for us to follow. We just need to trust God to provide them for us!

Jared Duran, Pastor, Young Adult Leader

DITCH THE SAVIOR COMPLEX

A good place to start is to ditch the savior or Messiah complex. I think Emma Bleker may have said it best, *"You should not have to rip yourself into pieces to keep others whole."* But for too many of us, this is exactly our reality. The graveyard of broken, jaded, and burned-out leaders is unfortunately very real. As I said, ministry is an amazing thing if we can survive it—and it's true. But we can survive it and even thrive in it if we give up trying to be everyone's Savior. Saviors tend to get crucified, and so will you if you persist in trying to be one.

In case you forgot, none of us died on a cross to forgive anybody's sin, and clearly we haven't been raised from the dead. Jesus is the one and only Savior and you're not. As hard as you may try, you can't save anybody, a fact I hope you've already figured out by now. People may want you to be their savior (they may not call it that), but it's a trap where everyone loses. And once you're in it, it is really difficult to escape. The savior complex is very subtle, and you don't notice it until you are deeply enthralled in it. Our job is to simply do everything we possibly can to help get people to the Savior and His name is Jesus!

I am not saying that you don't need to love and care for people—because you do and you must. You can give thirsty people a drink, but what they need is to find the source of that water for themselves with your help. Trying to be "all things to all people" is a dark hole that will never be filled. Eventually, it catches up to you in the form of panic attacks, depression, exhaustion, sleeplessness, disorientation, and various medical conditions. It doesn't have to be that way. You are not supposed to lose your life (or your soul) on the altar of ministry.

When we started our church in Colorado, my stress level grew due to the number of hours I spent counseling. Soon, people started to depend heavily on me. They believed that if they could just get Pastor Rick to pray for them, counsel them and tell them what to do, everything would be okay. My reputation grew as a counselor, (which was my specialty) but so did people's reliance on me. Soon I realized that there was only so much of me to go around and something needed to change. What had made me feel useful became overwhelming as it consumed the majority of my time and energy.

I had an encounter with a woman in our church helped bring things in perspective. This woman was in the hospital and requested a visit from me. She was in one of our small groups, and group members had regularly visited her to pray with her and offer encouragement. I was so proud of this small group, which was doing the very thing we had hoped would happen in a situation like this. Imagine my surprise when, upon my arrival in her hospital room, she said, "Pastor, thanks so much for coming. No one from the church has come to visit me here in the hospital!" *What?* I knew for a fact that at least a dozen different people from our church had visited her. But none of them counted because they were not me, the lead pastor.

Here's the deal: You are not responsible for people, but you are accountable to God for the people you lead. Catch that? They are His people, not yours. And it's not your job to stop people from sinning, make them love Jesus more, be free from addiction, faithfully serve God, or be happily married. We can provide help by providing support, resources and the tools they need to grow in these areas. I've known some pastors who actually keep a scorecard on people they've done weddings for who are still married. They wear it like a merit badge, as if the marriage survived because they did all the right things in preparing them. Conversely, I have seen other pastors lament and blame themselves when marriages blow up and end in divorce whom they spent hours counseling.

In Galatians 6:2, we are told, *"Carry each other's burdens, and in this way you will fulfill the law of Christ"* (NIV). But a few verses later we read, *"...for each one should carry their own load"* (Gal. 6:5). Does that seem like a contradiction? It's not. We are to come alongside people to support and encourage them and share their heartache's and burdens, but we can't take responsibility for them.

SURRENDER YOUR CAPE AND MASK

Fighting to protect and maintain your public image is like being on an endless treadmill to nowhere. Ditching the savior complex means not living up to impossible expectations. There was a time in leading our church that my image became too important to me —and impossible to maintain. A leader in our church gave me a book she had been reading called *No longer the Hero*. At first I thought to myself, "Are you giving this to me because you think I have some kind of hero complex?" Of course she did—and she was somewhat (okay, mostly) right! No longer the hero ... do you hear the ring of freedom in that? I do!

Fighting for an image is a curse, a noose around your neck. People who live to protect and build their persona or image, after a while they don't know the difference between their true self and false self. This is a battle we all face: Who I really am (and what I am striving to be) versus what I want others to think of me. This is why finding your identity deeply entrenched in Jesus is so critical from the outset. Fighting to keep our public image is like trying to keep a beach ball underwater. It takes all your attention and effort to do it. But one momentary lapse, and that beach ball bounces up for all to see.

In 2001, we had a very unfortunate moral failure on our staff at the height of our church's growth, and in the aftermath, our church began to steadily decline. I was disheartened and depressed by the whole ordeal and did not lead well for quite a while. It's hard to admit, but it's true. After 37 years in one church, I have come to realize that none of us leads well all the time, including you and me.

During this time, I was talking (lamenting actually) to Greg Thompson, a close pastor friend of mine from the Denver area. After listening to all my whining about the situation, he told me that I needed to quit worrying about my image and move on and start leading my church again. "*What, my image?*" I thought. "No way was I worried about that ... or was I?"

Turns out, he struck a nerve, one that would become a turning point for me. I came to see that my image was too important to me. I had prided myself that we had no moral failures, no church splits, no church decline, no major staff issues, etc. Through the years, I have now experienced all of that and more. It was actually a relief and quite liberating surrendering the image of the perfect pastor and leader. I gave up trying to be the hero (or the perfect pastor) because I wasn't and I didn't need to be. From that point on, I no longer tried to be the best at everything, which wasn't all that easy for me. I am super competitive and don't like losing at anything. (Once, Becky beat me in a video game, and I made her keep playing until I won.) I am no longer trying to be the hero but **strive to be the best I can be** in my current situation. Not the best husband or father, but the best one I can be in the stage of life I am in. The difference is subtle but important. I am so grateful to Greg for his willingness to tell me what I needed to hear that day. I'm not sure I could have received this from someone who I thought didn't care about me, but I knew he did. At the end of the day I am what I am by the grace of God—and so are you!

DELEGATE ... FOR YOUR SURVIVAL ... AND FOR THOSE YOU LEAD

Ditching the savior complex also means letting others lead. **You don't have to be the expert on everything.** That was where Moses was before he got some great counsel from his father-in-law of all people in *Exodus 18:13-23*. His father-in-law, Jethro, comes in at just the right time in verses 13-14:

> *The next day, Moses took his seat to hear the people's disputes against each other. They waited before him from morning till evening. When Moses' father-in-law saw all that Moses was doing for the people,* he asked, *"What are you really accomplishing here? Why are you trying to do all this alone while everyone stands around you from morning till evening?"* (NLT).

What a great question. Jethro comes from the outside of the situation and sees that Moses is exhausted and stressed out. He is also wearing out the people as nothing is actually being accomplished. **Leaders who do not delegate do not last very long**, and Moses wouldn't have either if not for Jethro's intervention. You may need to have someone do what Jethro did for Moses before you burn out.

Then Moses replied, *"Because the people come to me to get a ruling from God. When a dispute arises, they come to me, and I am the one who settles the case between the quarreling parties. I inform the people of God's decrees and give them his instructions"* (Exodus 18:15-16). Jethro told Moses what he needed to hear. What a great father-in-law!

We read in verses 17-18, *"'This is not good!' Moses' father-in-law exclaimed. 'You're going to wear yourself out—and the people, too. This job is too heavy a burden for you to handle all by yourself. Now listen to me, and let me give you a word of advice, and may God be with you. You should continue to be the people's representative before God, bringing their disputes to him. Teach them God's decrees, and give them his instructions. Show them how to conduct their lives'"* (NLT).

Then Jethro tells Moses to pick some capable people (just like in Acts 6) who fear God and are trustworthy and appoint them as leaders over groups of one thousand, one hundred, fifty and ten. Your ability to delegate is not only critical to your leadership but also to your emotional health and the well-being of those you lead. It's not optional!

In Ex. 18:22b-23, we get to see the outcome of a healthy story —all because of one father-in-law's wise counsel. "'*They will help you carry the load, making the task easier for you. If you follow this advice, and if God commands you to do so, then you will be able to endure the pressures, and **all these people will go home in peace**'*" (emphasis added). What great advice for Moses but also for us today.

LET OTHERS LEAD

I have discovered that great leadership is often demonstrated by empowering others to lead and realizing that you **don't always have to be an expert at everything**. (Go ahead—exhale.) An insecure pastor or leader will sometimes hold other strong and gifted leaders back because they feel threatened. I tried to recruit people who were more gifted, smarter, and better looking (hard to find!) than me. If you want to be a great leader, you must learn to delegate.

One of the challenges in releasing new leaders is that you can easily forget how inexperienced you were when someone gave you your first chance to lead. Over and over again I hear, "they aren't ready, they are not ready yet," even from some of my small group leaders whose job description was to raise up a new leader to start another group or take over the one they were in. Sometimes they were right and the next leader wasn't quite ready, but some times they were wrong and held potential leaders back unnecessarily.

There was one kinship leader couple whom I had asked for months why they were not releasing a particular couple to take the next step. They kept saying over and over again, "They have great potential, and are great people, but they are just not ready!" Exasperated, I finally blurted out (nicely), "Well, actually they are more ready (capable) than you were when I released you to lead your group!" I also reminded them that we typically want the next leader to be where we are now, not where we started. The lights went on and they finally got it, and soon after released them. This new leader couple turned out to be some of the best small group leaders we ever had and later joined our staff as small group pastors! In situations like this, I have discovered that sometimes there is an underlying fear in leaders that if they release someone and they fail, it would be their failure too. I think fear like this can be a major reason leaders have a hard time releasing others to lead.

I am what I am today because there were some leaders who took a risk and gave me a chance to do something I was not completely ready for. I am not talking about feeding people to the lions here. We do need to prepare people for the next step. On Paul's missionary journeys, there were times he had to move on and—ready or not—he picked people to take over and lead. There were also some who held me back for a season for my good, and I am also grateful for them as well. Timing is everything in delegation and team building! I bet when you think about it, you can remember a time when someone gave you a chance to do something "you were not ready for." How did that work out for you? Who are you taking a risk on?

It's *always* a risk to release someone into ministry, but it is so rewarding to see them step up in exciting ways. Now, you still need a thoughtful process for determining how to release leaders. Building your team, releasing leaders and hiring staff are some of the most important things you will do as a leader in whatever sphere of influence you serve. Finding the right people and then putting them in the right place at the right time is a recipe for success for any team. That was my philosophy in my football coaching years, and it worked. It is so rewarding when you believe in people who don't believe in themselves quite yet. It is so fun to call things out of people and see them come alive and step into the more God has for them. You can do this—and you need others to know they can do it too.

TAKE CARE OF YOURSELF

Sanjiv Yajnik, president of Capital One Financial Services, wrote this in an article for the Capital One blog called "Maximize Your Career Potential with These 7 Steps."

We tend to take care of everyone and everything around us (professionally and personally), and put ourselves last. But, physical and mental health is so critical to being successful. Let's take Formula One racing as an example. F1 racing is intense, and each team has hundreds of employees with various responsibilities that are critical to a successful race. Each competitor has a Team Principal, who is the primary decision-maker and the one held accountable for the overall success of the team. Before races, the Team Principal is responsible for managing the team and ensuring everything about the car is ready and optimized before race day. The Team Principal makes the call on when the driver takes a pit stop to change the tires, and is heavily relied on by the whole team to make the best judgment at every turn. So let's say there's a Team Principal who's running around and trying to handle everything alone leading up to race day, while hardly sleeping at night. Then, there's another Team Principal who hires good people, trusts them to do their jobs and is getting the rest needed to have a clear mind and provide the best guidance on race day. Which leader would you rather drive for? Taking time to care for yourself will pay massive dividends in the long run.

Did you know that according to the Centers for Disease Control and Prevention, nearly half of all adults will experience mental illness in their lifetime? And that number includes pastors. Taking care of yourself is your responsibility and you need to get help before you think you need it! Refuse to allow the "mental illness" tag to scare you off. Mental illness is no worse than any other illness, but unfortunately, there has been a lot of unfair stigma that pushes people, especially pastors, to keep silent and not get necessary help. Take proper medications for mental or emotional issues as you would for any physical infirmity you may have—and don't apologize.

Unfortunately, the church has been slow to recognize and validate this, especially in pastors. I can go to my church and share that I have leukemia, which I have, and I get a very sympathetic and loving response, which I've received. But what if I share that I am struggling with mental illness? I suspect that the response to my admission would be very different. Might you instead hear, "What? You are mentally ill? We need a new pastor." I hope that is not the case for you.

Young leaders, sometimes you might not be self-aware enough to know how you are actually doing, so you need the input from others who know you well. Don't trust yourself on this one. We can too easily lie to ourselves and think we are okay when we are not! So here is a big question for you. Is your pace sustainable? How is your soul? These may be the most important questions you can ask yourself as a young leader. I highly recommend *The Emotionally Healthy Leader* by Peter Scazzero, which has been very helpful to me and other leaders.

When you have an unsustainable rhythm in your life, your body may be the first to let you know. Pay attention to the signs you may be out of balance. Are you overweight, out of shape, not sleeping, tired all the time, stomach problems, headaches, panic attacks, etc.? Your body will many times tell you how you are really doing and that you need to take a break, see a doctor or get some rest. If you don't listen to it, your body will begin to unravel, even shut down and you will pay an unnecessary price for it.

Paul told the Corinthians that they were bought with a price, which is the blood of Jesus, and that their bodies were now the temple of the Holy Spirit and they were to glorify God with them. Think about it. Taking good care of your body is actually part of worshiping God. God will oftentimes use your body to speak to you. Listen to your body!

Gary Maura's Story

I met Gary at a pastor's retreat in South Carolina. As he shared some of the fallout from his time in ministry, I was captured by his transparency and openness about his struggles and we quickly developed a special connection. When I told him I was writing this book, I asked him what he would say to himself when he was 23 and he immediately answered, "Listen to your body. I regret that I didn't listen to mine and I paid a high price."

You've probably heard the statistics. Seventy percent of all pastors say they regularly fight depression. Fifty percent of pastors are so discouraged they would quit the ministry if they could afford to. Eighty percent of pastors believe the ministry has had a negative impact on their health and their families. And so on...

If you would've asked me in my twenties and thirties what I thought about the pastors who fell into those statistical categories, I would have said they were "losers." They must be unspiritual, denominational, career ministers, stuck in dead-end ministries. That could never be me.

If you would ask me now, at age sixty-two and after over thirty years of successful church planting and church growth, I would say "watch out" because pride goes before a fall.

I planted our church in 1990 with no people and no money, and it grew to one of the largest churches in our city. I remember looking out at four thousand people over one weekend and feeling pretty good about me, God, and the Bible.

After fifteen years of running and praying hard, I remember the signs of success and that God was truly with us. We had loads of people giving their lives to Christ. Families were being changed. We owned property and buildings, and had plenty of resources. We even had the ability to influence our elected leaders and community.

Little did I know that in just under five years, I would suffer a major burnout that would forever change my life and ministry.

While I was celebrating all the signs of spiritual success, I was ignoring all of the signs of a physical and mental breakdown. I was praying for vision and spending hours in my prayer closet to hear the still small voice of God, and all along God was shouting to me through my body.

Under the pressures of ministry, I had begun to develop chronic migraine headaches, insomnia, severe IBS, and a growing struggle with anxiety and stress that was taxing my mind and body. I ignored it for five years and took medication to power through. I especially loaded up on the weekends where I felt the pressure most acutely. I came to church late and stayed in the bathroom until it was time to preach. It never even occurred to me that God might be speaking to me through my body.

It turns out that ignoring physical and emotional warning signs for five years is not a wise ministry strategy. Things escalated, and I began having full-blown panic attacks while preaching. I had no idea what was happening to me, but I knew something was very wrong. It got to the point that I found myself in the fetal position at home on Sunday mornings begging God to take me to heaven and not to make me go to church.

God had finally gotten my attention. I confided in a pastoral counselor, and began the long process of getting the medical and emotional help I needed. I would like to tell you that I was healed and whole, and my life went back to normal, but that isn't what happened. Some injuries can leave you with a permanent limp and that is what I got. And some of the ways that we do life and ministry are never what God intended, and are simply unsustainable.

In the Bible, Elijah had a similar kind of burnout experience (read I Kings 19). Afterward, God provided a prescription that would become the blueprint for a newer, healthier life and ministry for me. God spoke to me through this passage, and these are the steps: 1. Rest your body. Elijah ate bread, drank water and slept. That's all he did over and over until he was healthy again. Take care of your mental and physical health, and listen *to your body. 2. Reorganize your life. Don't do life and ministry alone. Get help. Elijah went and found Elisha. Reorganize the way you do things because you can't carry the burden of ministry alone. 3. Renew your spirit. Hear the still small voice of God, and get away from the addiction to bigger and louder and greater things Let God gently lead you in green pastures and beside His still waters.*

I am in a much healthier place now as I have transitioned leadership of our church to a new generation of leaders, and today I have so much fun coaching and spending time with pastors at soul care retreats designed to help them live well and finish strong. And that is my hope for you as well.

Young leaders, I assume you are going to listen to God. I assume you are going to listen to your spirit. I assume you are going to listen to His Word. But I think you might miss another voice. Don't make the same mistake that I made. My advice is simple:Listen to your body. It just might be that God is trying to get your attention and shouting to you through your own body.

GaryMauro, Pastor, teacher, coach, GaryMauro.Com

SELF-LEADERSHIP

The biggest leadership challenge you will ever face—you guessed it—is *you*. Leaders go first in everything, so be the change you want to see in those you lead. Be the first partaker of the fruit so you can feed others. What you want to see others do needs to be what you do. When I looked at the strengths and weaknesses of my Fort Collins church, I often saw a reflection of myself both good and bad. It was not always a pretty picture but it was generally true. As I worked more on me and my stuff, I could see the benefits in our church and those around me. I wanted us to be a more praying church, which meant I needed to pray more than I was! I encouraged them to serve outside the church, so this led to me becoming a volunteer police chaplain which I did for twenty years. What do you need to work on to be the change that is needed in your church or ministry?

A CHALLENGE FROM AN OG

During my early days in Colorado, Charlie Patchen, who had recently retired after pastoring the largest church in our city, joined me in the Fort Collins Police chaplaincy program. After one of our chaplain meetings he told me very plainly, "I know young guys like you. You go, go, go and never stop filling up your life and you have no margins. Are you spending time with your kids? Do you have date nights? Are you taking real vacations? Are you treating ministry as a sprint or a marathon? With the pace you are on, I doubt you're going to finish well, if at all." Between being offended and convicted, as a young leader, I was rattled by this encounter because he was spot on in what he said. But how could he know? I could have blown him off, but what if he was right? What did I need to change?

As it turned out, we had young twin boys who needed more of me. And I was not taking vacations, rarely observed the Sabbath, struggled to find time for date nights, and remained fixated on the needs of my church, so much so that I could not see what was going on. Pastor Charlie certainly got my attention that day, and I began to implement some changes and put some boundaries in place (not all at once) that would eventually become new rhythms of my life, family, and ministry. Somehow he knew my pace was not sustainable.

Moving forward, I stopped answering my phone except for real emergencies on Monday and had other leaders step up to take those calls. So many times, people made their emergency mine. Most times, it could wait for a day or two. Thanks to Charlie, I realized that what I was doing was not good nor was it sustainable for the long haul. I'm so grateful he was willing to speak into my life at a critical junction before it was too late.

ON THE SHELF ... FOR MY OWN GOOD

Every leader has a season of being on the shelf and it can actually be a good thing. John Wimber did something to help me not lose my marriage, family, or church. He put me on the shelf after a breakthrough speaking moment in Frankfurt, Germany to over four thousand people, which made no sense to me at the time. I thought this was the beginning of more opportunities like this, but it wasn't meant to be. John cared enough about me and my marriage and family to push the pause button for me. I was disappointed—no, I was upset and hurt—but so grateful now as I look back on it because it worked.

After that major speaking moment, I went to John and "humbly" told him I was available for whatever he needed. It was code for I wanted to go on the speaking circuit with him. I cringe in writing this as I was so full of myself but didn't see it at the time. I can't imagine how stupid I looked to him. Instead of saying, "I want you to join my conference speaking team," he said, "Great, here is what I want you to do." I was expecting to hear him share about how we were going to travel together, but instead he said, "I want you to go home and build a great church in Fort Collins, love Becky, and be there for your kids." *And?* There was no *and* as he continued, "I don't want you to make the same mistakes I made and lose your family." He added, "Later you will pack your bags and travel the world [which I now have]. Until then, take care of yourself, and give your best to Becky, your boys and your church." During this time, I was personally not in a good place and should not have been traveling anyway. I am grateful that he cared more about me and my family than my speaking ability and ministry.

Out of this came my family vision: to grow and build a strong marriage with Becky, and have my boys love God, the church, each other, and us. If I did this, the church and any future ministry would take care of itself. So far, the above has become a reality after forty-three years of marriage and having a great relationship with my two adult sons. Ministry and church come and go, but relationships are forever. Even growing a church to over two thousand, traveling thirty countries, and launching churches and pastors over thirty-five times does not compare. Jesus said, "For what does it profit a man to gain the whole world and forfeit his soul?" (Mark 8:36 English Standard Version). " Very many ministry leaders have done just that. They gained notoriety, become famous and successful, and, yes, lost their souls—and so much more. Jesus closed by saying in verse 37, "For what can a man give in return for his soul?" How would you answer that?

BURY THE MYTH OF THE PERFECT FAMILY

One of the biggest challenges you might face as a young leader is the pressure of having the perfect family—which doesn't exist. Like it or not, some people will judge you by your family. Many pastors' kids struggle with having to live up to a special standard because their mom or dad is a pastor. I remember one time when someone came up to Becky to share a "concern" about our son's blue hair and how it might influence others teens. Becky immediately responded that she was the one who dyed his hair and how cool she thought it looked! She nipped this in the bud and made it clear that our boys did not have to live up to her standards. We had no more problems with her after this. Sometimes you have to stand your ground for your kids and allow them to be kids who are simply flexing their wings as they explore who they are and who they want to be. There is no perfect family, and you will never have one. So give up trying to have the perfect marriage or the perfect family, but focus on being the healthiest you can be.

So, how can we then do family within the fishbowl of ministry?

I grew up in the *Leave it to Beaver*, *Father Knows Best*, and *The Adventures of Ozzie and Harriet* era. *Ozzie and Harriet* was the first actual reality show as they "attempted" (I know you've probably never heard of them) to portray the "perfect" family and what a perfect family life looked like. It was more like a science fiction show as I look back on that impossible-to-duplicate "perfect" family that I wouldn't even want if I could have it. It was part of the facade of the times, projecting a false family image that nobody could live up to.

From 1952 to 1966, *The Adventures of Ozzie and Harriet* was a television staple, which may have preceded *Seinfeld* as the first show that was really about nothing. They were America's ideal fantasy couple in the 1950s. He was a bit goofy, never seemed to have a job, and was always puttering around the two-story Colonial house. She was an all-purpose mom who happily wore aprons most of the time and never seemed to leave the kitchen. Their sons, David and Ricky, were talented, virtuous and good-looking, two boys whose toughest problems seemed to be getting a date for the high school prom and asking Dad for the keys to the car.

The Nelson family, in real life, were hardly the Nelsons portrayed on television. As Kris Nelson Tinker, the former wife of Ricky Nelson, said on a documentary about the show: "I spent my whole life fighting the fairy tale.[1] First, trying to be it, then trying to tell the truth." (She shared about her and Rick's free fall from a seemingly perfect couple to one shattered by drugs and other demons.) And as her daughter Tracy Nelson said, "There's a huge discrepancy between what was real and what people think was real about the Nelson family and the people involved." Did you catch that? Discrepancy between what was real and what people thought was real.

Sadly, that is a picture I see too often in the church landscape today, something that desperately needs to change. The *Ozzie and Harriet* show was just that—a show. But we can put on a show for others, projecting one thing and being quite another. I was thinking that if character is so important to us, is there such a thing as family character? Are we the same on the outside as we are on the inside? Depending on the family you grew up in, it sounds scary, doesn't it? You might be thinking, "No way do I want anyone to know what really went on in my family," right?

Yet in the fishbowl of ministry, what are you to do when you can't live up to those unattainable expectations that others put on you? It becomes a big temptation to withdraw and hide your problems to protect your family from the judgment and scrutiny of others, instead of getting the help you need.

I have found that being flexible and adjusting to the various seasons of your life and ministry is crucial. Seasons like being single, newly married, having little kids, having kids in school, having teens, kids leaving home (and coming back!), becoming one of those empty nesters, and then you get to be an OG like me! There are seasons of ministry and church too. We also had to adjust our family rhythm to the seasons of our church. Something to remember about life's seasons? They don't last forever! Winters don't, nor does spring, summer, or fall. Sometimes it seems like the winter will last forever but it won't. Winter is just a season like the others, but you need to realize that you only have grace for the season you are in, not the one you wish you were in. In Colorado, after summer and early fall, it was time to put away the shorts (I loved wearing shorts) and get out the shovels and winter coats. Ready or not, winter was coming and I had to deal with it.

FIND YOUR FAMILY RHYTHM

Every family has a rhythm. Some are helpful, some not so much. What works for you might not work for me. We did find it helpful observing others who we felt were healthy families to glean from. Like us, every family needs to find one that works for them. What needs to be a higher priority than ministry? Your family, your marriage and your soul. God, family, and ministry is the right order, and it's easier to say than to actually do it. Young leader, it's not worth losing your family because of your ministry. You may still have a job, a salary, and a title, but it's really over. Remember what Jesus said in Mark 8:37, "For what will it profit a man if he gains the whole world, and loses his own soul? [37] Or what will a man give in exchange for his soul?" (NKJV). (In other words, what will we have left if we lose our family, health and relationships?) Translation: it's not worth it!

I have heard, read, and been told that family rhythms should look a certain way: Have breakfast all together, take the kids to school, be home when school is out, eat dinner at the same time every night. Then play some family games, read some stories and pray for each kid as they fall asleep. These are all great ideas for families and we implemented many of these. But this doesn't always work for everyone in our crazy culture today. Many work a swing or graveyard shift and have irregular hours. Then there are sports, music lessons, and other activities that come into play. Young leaders, you have to find what works best for you and your family in the various seasons of your life.

Becky and I found that some conventional understanding of family time as such did not always work for us. It did not fit our schedule, lifestyle and family situation. Between meetings, late appointments, boys' karate lessons and other sports, we needed to find out what worked for our family. We had to break with conventional ways because it did not work for us. We ate out a lot, went to sports bars mostly, and had great family times. I've heard the importance of family meals at home, but when we got home many nights, trying to figure out dinner, it added more stress to our busy family. I do not regret this as it worked for our family. But find what works for your family and refuse to listen to the expert nay-sayers. You need quality and quantity time with your family for sure, but you need to find a rhythm that works best for you to make that happen.

A WORD ABOUT BURNOUT

If you are feeling exhausted and sluggish and even simple tasks feel overwhelming to complete—or you find yourself so stressed out that you're quick to get angry or frustrated—you might be experiencing burnout. And burnout does not only affect you but also your family. You may not realize you've hit the wall until it's too late. You want to avoid crossing the line between "really tired" and "too exhausted to function." Alternatively, you might be the type of personality who likes to stay busy, and might not recognize when you're doing too much. Burnout also happens when your work or ministry life balance gets out of sync. This has been a common occurrence in the work place these last few years, with the rise in remote work and technology permeating our daily lives. Sometimes you just have to make yourself STOP working!

Many of us have become addicted-to-adrenaline rushes, and you may need some detoxing. I think that was sometimes true in my case. At times, I would be struggling with symptoms of burnout but then an adrenaline event would kick in and, like a drug, I would get the high before the next low came. Sometimes I would crash and often withdraw into my cave. I don't know what your cave looks like but mine was sleep, comfort foods (Krispy Kreme worked really well), and watching sports and news on TV —anything to veg out. The issue for some of us is that we stay in our cave until the next adrenaline high event calls us out and then we go back to our cave after it's over. It's a cycle for disaster.

The problem is that this cycle requires more and more adrenaline to get you back up on the horse. Pastors and leaders get this after speaking or having a creative strategy meeting or finishing a great conference. The Monday morning blues or gloom following the high of Sunday is very real as we head into our chosen cave. This swing from high to low will take its toll before long, not only on you, but on those around you. Being an adrenaline junkie is like any addiction—you need more and more to get you going and it becomes an endless cycle. And then, like Elijah, you can end up underneath a tree or in a cave, wishing you could die.

Some warning signs of burnout:

- Withdrawing from responsibilities
- Detachment, isolating yourself from others
- Using food, drugs, or alcohol to cope

- Taking out your frustrations on others
- Headaches
- Lack of sleep
- Chronic Fatigue
- Difficulty concentrating
- Emotional numbness
- An increasingly cynical outlook on life and ministry

SABBATHS: THE ANTIDOTE FOR BURNOUT

Burnout and sabbaths are linked. God doesn't burn out, but we do. He has called you and me to sabbath rest so burnout does not ruin your life.

> *"Remember the Sabbath day by keeping it holy. Six days you shall labor and do all your work, but the seventh day is a sabbath to the Lord your God. On it you shall not do any work, neither you, nor your son or daughter... For in six days the Lord made the heavens and the earth, the sea, and all that is in them, but he rested on the seventh day. Therefore the Lord blessed the Sabbath day and made it holy" (Exodus 20:8-11 NIV).*

We were not made just to work, work, work! God created us to need a rest! Too often we act like God doesn't know what He is doing when He tells us to rest. Do you listen to people around you who tell you to slow down and take a break or go on vacation? Remembering the Sabbath is one of the big ten. God told us to keep it holy! What does that mean? Merriam-Webster defines "holy" as "devoted entirely to the deity or the work of the deity."[2] I think it means to not minimize, taint, or dismiss the Sabbath. To keep it holy means to use it as God intends. This is a challenge for anyone like me who has attention-deficit disorder.

Jesus even emphasized this in Mark 2:27-28: *"Then Jesus said to them, 'The Sabbath was made to meet the needs of people, and not people to meet the requirements of the Sabbath. So the Son of Man is Lord, even over the Sabbath!'"* (NIV).

Many miss the point on the purpose of the Sabbath. The Pharisees made it a religious requirement and added their own spin on what was required and allowed. Jesus challenged this numerous times, especially when He was attacked for healing a man on the Sabbath in the synagogue. Consider what the writer of Hebrews had to say about this:

> *God's promise of entering his rest still stands, so we ought to tremble with fear that some of you might fail to experience it. For this good news—that God has prepared this rest—has been announced to us just as it was to them. But it did them no good because they didn't share the faith of those who listen to God... So there is a special rest still waiting for the people of God. For all who have entered into God's rest have rested from their labors, just as God did after creating the world. So let us do our best to enter that rest. But if we disobey God, as the people of Israel did, we will fall (Hebrews 4:1-2, 9-11* NLT*).*

It takes faith and courage to enter God's rest, to let go and admit we are not superhuman. It also means giving up control, which is hard for many of us to do. God did not rest because He was tired but because He knew that we get tired, so he set in motion just what we needed—a sabbath rest. We pay a heavy price when we ignore the commands of God, like the Sabbath, which is always for our good. I have heard many leaders admit they need a break or a sabbath but don't take it. Some say, "I would love to rest and take some time off and have a Sabbath, but I just don't have enough time." When our lives get full, the first thing to go is typically our time for rest. With a sabbath rest, you can actually get more done in six days than you will accomplish in seven. Try it and watch how God will multiply your time when you take a Sabbath once a week.

Betsy de Cruz shares some very helpful thoughts on the importance of the biblical Sabbath:

The word "Sabbath" is related to a Hebrew root that means "to cease" or "to stop." God commanded His people to cease from their labor, so they could rest, refresh, and refuel. After leaving Egypt they were no longer required to work non-stop like slaves. God gave them the gift of rest, a day to cease from working and to honor Him. Many dread Mondays not only because it's hard to get back into the swing of work, but also because we exhaust ourselves all weekend long. God knows about our "never stop and do it all" tendency therefore he gifted us with the Sabbath. All of God's laws are for our benefit whether we realize it or not. Since God included the Sabbath in the 10 Commandments, He must have thought it was pretty important. No one can work 24/7, right? Perhaps today's trend of online working makes setting aside time to rest more difficult, yet more important than ever. When we take time to refuel spiritually, we're better equipped to deal with challenges and trials that will always be part of our lives. I do not believe it matters when you choose to have a sabbath but you need to make room in your life for it. I know many pastors use Monday for their sabbath rest day since Sunday can be a pretty intense work day for us. If your job requires you to work on Sunday, ask the Lord for creativity and discipline to set aside another Sabbath time during your week.

Start by setting aside one day a week when you put your work down and focus on you and God. Take a walk, go on a bike ride, hike a trail, go for a swim, read a novel or some inspiring blogs or parts of the Bible. And ditch your phone!

Also, think about mini sabbaths where you take an hour out of every day, or a micro Sabbath, with fifteen minutes here or there where you take a short walk, or take a moment where you invite God into the "now" moment of your life. At any time—morning, noon or night—you can tune into the God who created the universe. And you won't get a busy signal either or be put on hold! God is always closer than you realize. Maybe the operative word is *stop*. For a day, an hour or even ten minutes, just stop. You have probably guessed that I am not good at this sabbath thing, but I am still working on it. I would certainly tell myself when I was a young leader—and even now—to stop and make sabbaths a regular rhythm in my life.

I sometimes jokingly told my wife, who is really good at carving out time for daily devotions and connecting with God, to "tell God 'hi' for me when you see Him." Funny in a sense, but actually quite sad when you think of it, as I was relying on her God connection rather than my own.

Years ago, there was a time when I was not doing well and felt a disconnect with God. At one point I thought I heard God say something that rattled my cage. "Rick, I miss you!" That was it: "I miss you!" How could God miss me? No way could that be true. It was wild to think that God, the creator of the universe, actually misses spending quality time with me. I realized that this was not just about my needing to be close to God, but His desire to be close to me. That was a game-changing moment for me. Young leader, might God say something similar to you? Is your pace more like a chicken with his head cut off? When was the last time you invited God into your right-now life? Think about this. God's eyes are never off of me or you. That is good news for sure unless we are doing stupid stuff we don't want Him to see. God sees it all, and some of what He sees breaks His heart. I do not want to break God's heart, and it motivates me to live in such a way that would be honoring to Him.

WHAT FILLS YOUR CUP?

Typically, we don't stop long enough to answer this question. What things or people give you life? I had never heard of that expression before a friend asked me that. I didn't know how to answer, but it got me thinking. I need relationships that give me life where I can let down my guard and not be "on"—and you do too. We all need someone who is safe, someone we can talk about anything (or nothing) with, knowing that they will hold no judgment. John Borman is one of those people in my life. We have been friends for forty years and have a give-and-take relationship. Every time we are together, I feel refreshed and so does John. We all need friendships that are reciprocal like this.

As leaders, it is easy to get isolated as we continually pour ourselves out to others, but who does that for us? You can't keep giving and giving without receiving or your soul will dry up and die.

I believe we need three key relationships as a leader. First, we need those we lead and pour into their lives. Second, those who are peers and it's a mutual give-and-take relationship. Third, we need those who pour their lives into us and need nothing in return. Put another way, I need relationships where it's all about you, another where it's all about us, and one where it's all about me. I think God wants to give you all three to help sustain you for the long haul.

Do you have these types of relationships in your life? To stay healthy and balanced, I think it's really important to have all three. Like many leaders, most of my relationships were with those whom I led. I also had some peer relationships with pastor friends from other churches, but having someone who was just there for me without any strings attached has been much harder to come by.

FIND GOD AS YOUR HIDING PLACE

"You are my hiding place; you will protect me from trouble and surround me with songs of deliverance" (Psalm 32:7 NIV).

Ultimately, we need to go to the One who can feed our soul like no other. As much as you and I need life-giving relationships, only God can fill the cup of your soul. Like Elijah, it's not the wind or the earthquake but the small still voice we need to hear.

We can't and won't hear it when we are always on the go and never stop. Instead of running yourself ragged, why not run to Him instead? You won't do that unless you really believe in your heart of hearts that you personally matter to God more than anything—and you do! It's a journey of discovery with you and God, but it won't happen if you are constantly on the move and never slow down. As you slow down, begin to listen to the deepest part of your being. And remember that God is your hiding place —go there! He is the one who fills your cup that overflows to those around you. Healthy life, relationships and ministry comes out of the overflow of our communion with our Papa God!

As you go to God, He will teach you to love and care for yourself—body, soul and spirit. Situations may leave you feeling overwhelmed, but it's not the end. Rest if you need rest, cry if you are grieving, but don't stay in that place of weariness. God is saying, "Come, and I will restore you, My strength will become your strength and you will rise again. Cast your cares upon Me, for I care for you!" In Matthew 11:28, Jesus said, *"Come to **me**, all of you who are weary and carry heavy burdens and I will give you rest"* (NLT, emphasis added). The rest we get from God is real rest that goes deep into our soul. How does that sound?

QUESTIONS FOR THE HEART

1. Where is your hiding place? Do you have a special time and place to be alone with God?

2. Are there signs of burnout in your life?

3. Is your present pace of life sustainable? What needs to change?

4. Are you practicing sabbaths? Mini sabbaths? When will you start?

5. Do you have someone you can share anything with, the good, bad or ugly?

6. Do you have any meaningful relationships apart from ministry? Describe.

7. Do you have all three key relationships described above? Explain.

ELEVEN
KEEP SHORT ACCOUNTS

NOTHING IS MORE destructive and detrimental to your life and ministry than unforgiveness and bitterness. It's a powerful ministry-killer. Keeping short accounts is essential if you are to have a long and prosperous ministry. Being a leader guarantees that you will get hurt and offended along the way, but the critical piece is not so much the offense as how you respond to it. It will decide your future. To hold a grudge against someone is like binding a chain to your soul. Bitterness is like putting poison into a cup, drinking it, and waiting for your enemy to die. Bitter leaders tend to gather bitter followers. If you want bitterness to not root itself in your church or ministry, you need to first get it out of you. Forgiveness is the key that unlocks the promises of God for your life.

JOSEPH: BETRAYED BY HIS BROTHERS

Have you ever wondered how Joseph avoided bitterness after all he went through? If anybody had the right to be bitter it was Joseph right? Wrong! At the end of his story, we read Joseph's perspective on what happened to him: "You plotted evil against me, but God turned it into good, in order to preserve the lives of many people who are alive today because of what happened" (Genesis 50:20 GNT). Though he forgave them, he did not let them off the hook for what they had done. He looked at them right in the eyes and made the choice to forgive them. At the same time, he refused to minimize the hurt and pain they had caused him. I find it interesting that Joseph said this to his brothers when he had absolute power to get even and exact revenge. This is called mercy, and Jesus said something about this later in the Sermon on the Mount. Matthew 5:7 says: "God blesses those who are merciful, for they will be shown mercy" (NLT). **Mercy is not giving people what they deserve but giving them what they need.** That is what Jesus did for us and commands us to do to others.

If you were in Joseph's shoes, could you forgive your brothers for throwing you in a well and selling you into slavery launching your life into a downward spiral? If Joseph had wallowed in bitterness, his life probably would have been ruined and we would have a completely different end to the story. The only way to avoid bitterness in this world is to find contentment and solace in God alone. That is what Joseph did, and it worked for him and can work for you as well.

FACING MY BITTERNESS

Forgiving my stepfather and my mother was a long journey, but in the end, it has unhooked me from past hurts and freed me (and my family) to fully embrace and experience the life Jesus offered me.

My mom raised me by herself until I was seven when she married my stepdad, who was a professional gambler. Their relationship could only be characterized as very tumultuous and violent. There were many fights (both verbal and physical), and I felt pretty powerless to stop them. There were multiple times that the police were called, but in those days nobody seemed to care and no one was put in jail for things like that. I might add that my mom was just as violent as my stepdad and could usually hold her own. When I was around 10, I remember one big confrontation when Mom was throwing things and attacked my stepdad with a kitchen butcher knife. The next minute, my stepdad knocked my mom down. I jumped on him, but he threw me to the floor. Mom went crazy before the police finally showed up. I vowed that night that one day when I was bigger and stronger, I would make him pay for what he did.

An opportunity to get even with my stepdad arose years later just after I had given my life to Christ. I had made a routine phone call to my mom, who had long since divorced him, and my stepdad was over at her house and they were in the middle of a fight with blood-curdling screams. All my pent-up rage from over the years poured out as I left work and headed to her house to deal with him. But on the way there, I stopped by my girlfriend's house. She calmed me down, convincing me to call again before going after him. When I called, I found out it was not as bad as it seemed; everything was okay—but I wasn't. Where did all this anger and rage come from? I thought, *"I'm a Christian now and this isn't right."* As a result, I realized that the business I needed to do was between me and God, and it was time to forgive my stepdad.

That night, I made the choice to forgive Bob Pettigrew. I asked God to give me his heart for him and help me see him through His eyes. That night changed everything as I began reaching out to him. Later on, I had the privilege of not only leading him to Jesus but also officiating his memorial service. When he died, I had nothing but love in my heart for him. What a close call as bitterness was knocking at my door seeking to ruin the rest of my life, but I chose to not open it by forgiving my stepdad. But he wasn't the only one I had to forgive. I needed to forgive Mom.

DEALING WITH MOM ISSUES

Mom never bonded with any of her kids; she had a hard time expressing love of any kind. She was quite the wild teenager and totally unprepared to be a mom. She continued to struggle being a mom into her twenties. She was emotionally and verbally explosive, something she probably learned while growing up in a very troubled home, complete with a violent alcoholic father and a scolding mother who showed little, if any, affection. I came to realize that my mom was trying to do the best she could, but her best was not always good for us.

Not long after Becky and I had twin boys, we stopped bringing them to any holidays because it typically exploded into chaos. Some of my most painful times with her were when she constantly berated and shamed me for anything that went wrong with my brothers whom she had abandoned for a relationship with her lifetime partner Eileen. They were 13 and 15 years old at the time, and I was suddenly responsible for raising them, something I was not equipped to do. Over time, I realized I had built up a lot of resentment because of all this and so much more.

MOM COMES TO CHURCH—OH NO!

Years later, my mom and Eileen moved to Fort Collins and started coming to our church—and it was a huge turning point for all of us. Actually, it was life changing!

One Sunday morning at church, just before I was going up to speak, I greeted Mom and heard these words for the first time in my life: "I love you, and I am so proud of you." As she hugged me, I became stiff as a board, thinking that as a 60-year-old, it was way too late for this love stuff from her. I thought to myself, "I am happy to help and take care of you and Eileen, but that's it." Then something happened as I heard a voice in my head (it was God) say, "Stop punishing your mom and let her love you." I gasped and was stunned. My first response was denial: "I am not punishing her!" Then I heard God say, "And I want you to start loving Eileen too." This was a huge turning point in my life. I still am not sure how I had the composure to speak that morning, but from that point on, I not only forgave my mom, but I also started allowing her to love me. I stopped punishing her and Eileen, something I did not realize I had been doing.

As a result, both of their lives were dramatically changed, but no more than mine or Becky's. We began to celebrate both their birthdays, bought them a home, helped them financially, took them out to eat at least once a week, and got fully involved in their lives as they were now in their eighties. Becky was the real hero here as she was so supportive, and treated my mom and Eileen as if they were her own mom. They both died a few years apart, but we cared for them to the end and led their memorial services with much love in our hearts.

I can't understate the amount of healing I received from all this. What started as a choice ended with a deep love and affection for my mom. The healing power of forgiveness is so real, and I am fighting back tears as I write this. It's never too late to forgive and do the right thing—never! You do not want to carry the baggage of past offenses and hurts into your leadership, ministry, or life.

As I forgave Mom and my stepdad, it broke off my chains and stopped a generational curse from being passed on to my two sons. It's counterintuitive, but we become what we hate and become like those to whom we are embittered. Kids really do follow in your footsteps. They hate what you hate. Ever notice that? You are not just fighting for your future but also for theirs. When you forgive, the chains come off and the forgiveness releases tremendous freedom and blessings to you and your offspring. As I walked in forgiveness toward my mom and Eileen, I saw them come alive just like my stepdad did. It was all beyond anything I could have imagined.

REFUSE BITTERNESS, SEEK PEACE

It's important that we refuse to become bitter. We tell those we lead that they need to forgive and reject bitterness, but it needs to start with us. Leaders go first—and this arena is no different. Forgiveness for leaders means taking an honest look at your past and being willing to deal with painful issues and offenses. Unresolved hurts and offenses don't magically go away, and denial drives them underground even further, affecting every area of our lives. This isn't something you can do on your own; instead, you need to rely on the grace and power of the Holy Spirit. You begin by going to God and pouring out your heart and soul to Him—every hurt you've held onto—and ask Him for the grace to forgive.

The writer of Hebrews tells us to make every effort, meaning to do whatever it takes to live at peace with those around us. Not just a little nod here or there but going the extra mile like Jesus told us to do. *"Make every effort to live in peace with all men and to be holy; without holiness no one will see the Lord. See to it that no one misses the grace of God and that no bitter root grows up to cause trouble and defile many"* (Hebrews 12:14-15 NIV).

Then we are told that bitterness cuts us off from God's grace. Now just think about that for a moment. We miss the grace of God because we choose our bitterness over Him? That's a losing choice for sure. And that bitterness is like a contagious disease that creates havoc not just for you but also for those around you.

Ever notice how bad news travels fast? When a bitter root grows deep inside you, every part of your life is affected—like that vine we love to plant in our gardens that grows and grows until it takes over and covers everything. Bitterness is not worth it and needs to be cut off at the root. That means that seeds of resentment, offense, and wounds must be dealt with early and often. The fight against bitterness may be the biggest fight you will face in your life and ministry, but it's a battle worth fighting.

DON'T LET THE DEVIL IN

I have heard many teachers talk about how demons can infiltrate your life in various ways, but I have found only one verse that tells us how the devil gets into our lives.

Ephesians 4:26-27 says: *"In your anger do not sin. Do not let the sun go down while you are still angry, and do not give the devil a foothold"* (NIV). When we hold grudges and unforgiveness, we create ledges in our life for the devil to live on. When we forgive, that ledge disintegrates and the devil has nowhere to stand. So, we've got to deal with our bitterness and unforgiveness and not let it corrode our hearts. It's a choice...mine and yours.

It won't go away until you choose forgiveness over offense, revenge or bitterness.

Paul continues in verses 31-32: *"Get rid of all bitterness, rage and anger, brawling and slander, along with every form of malice.* ***Be kind and compassionate to one another, forgiving each other, just as in Christ God forgave you.***"

Paul doesn't say to get rid of some or most of your bitterness, rage and anger, but all of it. Then he gives the antidote to dealing with bitterness: kindness, love, compassion and forgiveness. How should we forgive? In the same way and manner that Jesus has forgiven us. We receive forgiveness we did not deserve and so we offer forgiveness to others who don't deserve it either. Paul doesn't say think about it; he says do it!! Forgiveness for leaders and pastors needs to be a constant and ongoing spiritual discipline.

Young leaders, forgive early and forgive often. Watch out for those secondhand offenses. They can sneak up on you, take you out, and they are hard to get over. Finally, remember that forgiveness is *not* a feeling; it's a choice, a healing choice that can change your life forever. If you wait until you feel like forgiving, you probably never will.

LET YOURSELF OFF THE HOOK

Forgive yourself because God already has. As Christ has forgiven you, you need to forgive others. But don't forget to forgive yourself. You can have a root of bitterness toward yourself, which is tragic and hard to extract. Getting free begins by accepting God's forgiveness once and for all and then forgiving yourself. You can't forgive yourself if you have not truly received God's forgiveness first. One might say, "If God hasn't forgiven me, why should I?" Well, He has and so should you.

What does receiving God's forgiveness look like? First John 1:9 tells us: *"But if we confess our sins to him, he is faithful and just to forgive us our sins and to cleanse us from all wickedness"* (NLT). I love the forgiveness part here, but we cannot forget about the need to get cleansed from the effects of our sin. Cleansing is what takes away the shame of our past. Too many leaders are driven because they are trying to atone in some way for their past sins. You can't lead if you keep carrying around all your junk from the past because sooner or later it will get dumped on those you lead. Penance (paying for your sin) is not an exercise Jesus puts on you —but "religion" will be happy to immerse you in it. Did Jesus atone for your sin or not? He did his part and now it's up to you to do yours. Young friends, it's time to let go of those chains you might be carrying from your past. Accept His forgiveness and cleansing once and for all, giving Him all your baggage.

Forgiving yourself is the doorway to loving yourself, which we are commanded to do in Mark 12:30-31:

> Jesus replied, *"The most important commandment is this: 'Listen, O Israel! The Lord our God is the one and only Lord. And you must love the Lord your God with all your heart, all your soul, all your mind, and all your strength.' The second is equally important: 'Love your neighbor as yourself.' No other commandment is greater than these"* (NLT).

You love yourself by starting to forgive yourself. You can actually be bitter toward yourself—which may be the hardest part to overcome. Someone once told me that bitterness toward others releases anger and rage whereas bitterness toward self leads to deep depression and self-hate. Self-bitterness is debilitating and also creates space for the devil to torment and shame you even more. Sometimes the devil doesn't have to shame you or beat you up because you are doing such a good job yourself. Self-hate leads to all sorts of destructive behavior. "I hate me so I will destroy my life and everything that is dear to me." Friend, Jesus is your advocate when the evil one continuously brings accusations against you. First John 2:1-2 needs to get planted in our minds. *"My dear children, I am writing this to you so that you will not sin. But if anyone does sin, we have an advocate who pleads our case before the Father. He is Jesus Christ, the one who is truly righteous. He himself is the sacrifice that atones for our sins—and not only our sins but the sins of all the world"* (NLT).

THE WOUNDS OF A FRIEND ...

Betrayal is quite another thing and very difficult to move past. Psalm 55:12-14 (NLT) says, *"It is not an enemy who taunts me—I could bear that. It is not my foes who so arrogantly insult me. I could have hidden from them. Instead, it is you—my equal, my companion and close friend. What fellowship we enjoyed as we walked together to the house of God."*

Peter or Judas—who hurt Jesus more? I wonder. Every leader has their Peter and some will have a Judas, too. Sooner or later, some level of betrayal will be a part of your journey too. Bitter or better—it's up to you. You can let it make you better, but you have to choose it. You can be like Joseph who kept his heart clean through it all, which made it possible for God to use him in extraordinary ways. He refused to allow bitterness to destroy his future and it would have. **You can't control what others do or**

don't do to you. But you can control how you respond—and that decides your future, not the offense.

When people reject and abandon us, the door to bitterness can swing wide open if we are not careful. Jesus knows what it feels like to be abandoned: Gethsemane, cross, and many who ceased to follow Him. When your friends turn against you (and some might), you have a decision to make. Will you allow that to take you out and stop you from pursuing your calling and mission, or will you "pick up your cross" and press on in spite of it?

When our church plant reached the early milestone of 200 regular attendees, some of those closest to me became very insecure and uncomfortable with all the new people coming to our church. Some drew back and complained, "Why do you need us with all these new folks coming?" In one particularly hard conversation with a key friend and leader, I said, "Why don't you stand outside our church next Sunday, and when the number is too many, you tell them they are not welcome because you are uncomfortable and don't want them here." He got the point, but sadly it was the beginning of the end for many who began leaving. It was heartbreaking.

They could not rejoice in what God was obviously doing in and through our new church. I realized later on that the real issue for some was that they did not have the same access to me as they used to with so many new leaders joining our team. So, I had a choice. Give in to my friends' wishes or continue to open our doors and lives to new people whom God was bringing our way. It was the hardest decision I had made to that point, but I know looking back it was the right one. We doubled to over 400 in the next year with many stepping into leadership roles and hundreds of people coming into relationship with Jesus. At the end of the day, giving God what He wants is our only option, though it will cost you and is not going to be a popular one.

You and I will not give an account before God for what people wanted. Can you imagine if Moses gave in to the whims of the Israelites in the wilderness who wanted to go back to Egypt because they didn't have enough meat? Yes, of course it hurt to have many of my closest friends vote *no* on me and the direction of our church. For some, I really think it may have boiled down to a pioneer versus homesteader issue. Many of the people who launch a new church are the pioneers, but when the "settlers" arrive, the pioneers get restless and seek new horizons. I did not think losing some of my closest friends was part of the leadership equation, but it was and will be for you as well.

For a while I beat myself up trying to figure out what I was doing wrong, but **saying goodbye to friends and hello to strangers became my reality.** This is true for leaders of growing churches and organizations. From the outset, I told God plainly that my skin was not thick enough for this job, but I couldn't get Him to agree. Over time, I did get more thick-skinned but my heart never did, which is why I was able to lead our church for 37 years. Proverbs 4:23 says, *"Guard your heart above all else, for it determines the course of your life"* (NLT). That's the issue. It's not about whether or not you are thick-skinned; it's about keeping your heart open to God and to those He sends your way.

BLESS THOSE WHO LEAVE

When people reject you and turn away from you, bitterness will try to work its way into your heart. In today's church landscape, people vote with their feet. I know pastors who, out of frustration and anger, sometimes even curse them as they leave. And to top it off, they also take it out on those who are still there!

What if you take a different approach and decide to bless those who leave for whatever reason—keeping the door open for God's blessing on you and your church? Young leaders, you are not in the people-keeping business, but the people-building business. John Wimber stressed how we need to understand that sooner or later everyone leaves—one way (they decide to move on) or the other (they leave for heaven). **You can lament over those** who leave, or you can choose to give yourself to those who are still there. This has been a saving grace in my life, choosing to pour into people again and again knowing they too will leave someday.

PEOPLE ABANDONED JESUS TOO

While teaching in the synagogue in Capernaum, Jesus' metaphor about eating His flesh and drinking His blood was taken literally by some, and many began deserting Him.

We pick up the story in John 6:66-68 (NLT): *"At this point many of his disciples turned away and deserted him. Then Jesus turned to the Twelve and asked, 'Are you also going to leave?' Simon Peter replied, 'Lord, to whom would we go? You have the words that give eternal life.'*"

What a moment as Jesus asks the twelve if they are leaving too. An atmosphere of rejection and abandonment was in the air. The text here says these were some of his disciples (not strangers) who turned away that day, but it did not stop Jesus from continuing to invest in those who were still there! Although most abandoned Jesus just after He was arrested, I believe He did not regret pouring His life into them day after day. When you invest in the lives of those you lead, you can (and should) rejoice whether they stay or move on. They take what you have given, and that is part of your lasting fruit. Again, it's not about who stays or goes but what you do with them while they are with you. There was one couple who left our church, and years later unbeknownst to me, ended up being the lead pastors of a church in California. You never know the impact you have in people's lives, but it's so rewarding when you do. This principle may be the most important part of helping me stay the course all these years. You never lose when you bless people and keep bridges down so they can return if they choose.

"I DON'T GET FED HERE"

Get ready cuz it's coming your way! One complaint leaders hear that cuts to the quick and causes great pain is "I don't get fed here." Gut check: How do you respond when you hear this? It's one of the common "drive-by guiltings" leaders get. I hear this from people coming to us and leaving us. Leaving because they are not being fed or coming because they were not being fed elsewhere. It feels like an endless treadmill sometimes.

John Wimber humorously addressed this issue, which is a complaint almost as old as time itself. Irritated, he said, "The Bible is the menu, not the meal. To study and fill up notebooks is not what it means to be fed. Doing what the Bible says is the meal. How much more do you want to know that you are not doing?" More information, more Greek, more of what you have never heard before aren't components of the meal. To go away after a seminar or teaching feeling like you were fed is like going to a restaurant and chewing up the menu declaring that you have had a great meal.

James 1:22 says, *"But be doers of the word, and not hearers only, deceiving yourselves"* (English Standard Version). Being a doer is where life is. As long as you feast on the menu, you will never be satisfied no matter how much of it you digest. The irony of all this is that we had people coming to our church saying they were not being fed at their last church while, at the same time, people were leaving our church saying the same thing. Our response? In the spirit of Luke 23:34, forgive and bless them, for they know not what they are doing.

Another hurtful phrase relates to Hebrews 5:12-14 where spiritual maturity is likened to meat versus milk. We leaders hear, "I want the meat and all I get around here is milk!" Everyone seems to have their own idea of what it means to have "meat." It might be using the Greek or focusing on controversial issues, doctrines, theologies, or difficult and obscure passages of the Bible. For sure we need to move on from the elementary teachings as the Bible encourages us to do, but the goal is to learn more so we can do more. Wimber added this poignant response to such grumbling: "Then here's what you do. Go out into the streets and have a drunk throw up on you. The meat is in the streets!" I never forgot that. The meat is when you give your life away to others. You are never more alive than when you give your life to others. As you do this, you will be well fed as you enjoy the meat of doing God's Word.

When Jesus forgave Peter, the ramifications of that moment echoed throughout history. It saved Peter's life and his future. Peter knew he had done the unthinkable in denying the Lord not once but three times, not to mention abandoning Him when Jesus needed him most. He saw it as unforgivable (it wasn't!), and it was over for him. Peter was certain Jesus was done with him, but he soon discovered that with God it's never over until it's over. Ashamed, Peter wasn't going to seek out Jesus after all he had done.

Jesus took the initiative and went to Peter on the shore of the Sea of Galilee and intruded on Peter's breakfast meal. In John 21, we read that Jesus asked Peter three times if he loved Him. By the third time, Peter was pretty shaken up. "Yes, I love you." I think shame was all over Peter at this moment, and Jesus was taking it off of him layer by layer.

He had denied the Lord three times, and now he was affirming his love for Jesus three times. Jesus' love for Peter was one thing, but he probably assumed that he was no longer on the team. " Then the answer came with new marching orders: *"Feed my sheep"* (John 21:17 NIV). After all that, Jesus invited him—just like that first day—to again follow Him. And Peter followed Jesus from that day forward without the chains of guilt and shame around him and the rest is history.

What an important lesson for us. Though we are faithless, He remains faithful because He cannot and will not deny who He is. We are all flawed like Peter, but we must remember that God's love is bigger than our flaws.

RECONCILIATION? OR RESTORATION? ... OR BOTH?

Reconciliation *and* restoration should always be our goal, but restoration is not always possible because bridges have been burned or blown up along the way. I knew a woman who was sexually abused by her dad as a child and came to a point in her life when she made the healing choice to forgive him. But there was no way she would ever allow him to be with her children. At one point her father said, "If you have really forgiven me, then why can't I see my grandkids?" Her answer was swift, "Yes, I have forgiven you, but I don't trust you to be around my family."

Forgiveness and reconciliation are one thing, but restoration is quite another. This woman had personally forgiven her father, but the relationship was not restored. You can forgive someone and be reconciled with them, but that does not mean things go back to the way they were. Forgiveness does not automatically take away the consequences of our actions (or theirs) as this abusive father discovered. You can forgive someone for the horrific things they have done without subjecting yourself or your family to more potential trauma and abuse. Sometimes we prematurely rush to restore. You can forgive someone for abusive behavior and, at the same time, create boundaries to cut off opportunities for it to happen again. Don't be too quick to confuse the two and try to restore prematurely.

Forgiving does not equal trusting. You can forgive someone who has done awful things, but you don't have to trust them and you shouldn't! Trust needs to be earned over time, and it really does take awhile, sometimes a long time. Consequences are a part of it too. Many people who are forgiven and fully reconciled to God are still in prison, not married any more, or not in ministry because they are experiencing the consequences of their choices. All sin is the same before God and forgivable, but sins have various levels of consequences that are clearly stated in the Bible. You can be forgiven and reconciled but not restored to the life you had before. Sometimes all three are possible, sometimes not. Always strive for forgiveness, reconciliation and restoration whenever possible.

WHEN THEY WON'T FORGIVE YOU

When you fall short of someone's expectations, let someone fall through the cracks, or have to make a hard decision that costs someone their livelihood, it causes hurt and offense. You can be remorseful, repentant and try to make amends, but some will refuse to forgive you. I have experienced the pain of this a few times over the years; it is really hard when you try everything but to no avail. I have a tough time with unresolved conflict, like most people, but sometimes you need to face the fact that reconciliation and resolution are not going to happen and you have to move on. Sometimes, you never get to find out what you have done wrong. If your goal is to never offend anyone, you need to find something else to do with your life.

When people won't forgive you, it stings. And, yes, it's hard to push through. So, what do you do when it happens? First, you go to God and confess whatever part you had in the situation and embrace His love and forgiveness. Second, you go to the person and try your best to reconcile. Third, realize that you have no control over how people respond or don't respond to you. What you do control is how you respond to those who have hurt you, but also to those who refuse to forgive you for whatever offenses they may have against you. Fourth, you let it go and move on!

A couple who were among some of our closest friends that we had on staff became very offended by some choices I made during a particularly hard season when I was not leading well. Becky and I made multiple overtures to them, but it has not been reciprocated and so we have had to let it go as we continually pray for God's blessing on their lives. At the same time, we remain open to the possibility that someday we can find a way to be friends again. One of the keys to what God has done in my life and ministry is my determination to lean into God's empowering grace to forgive, let go of grudges and resist bitterness to root itself in my heart—and I encourage you to do the same.

SHAME OFF YOU

For too much of my life I have had to fight off shame. Shame comes in multiple forms. It may be from the way you were born, your upbringing, your parents, your ethnicity, school or sports. Shame also appears through our failures and disappointments, the things done to us and things we have done to ourselves and others. Maybe it's because of times we did not stand up to a bully, or perhaps we quit or we gave up on something or someone, like a marriage. It's like carrying around a giant bag of weights.

You need to throw off everything that hinders or has stopped you from running the race God has chosen for you, especially your guilt and shame. God has forgiven you and cleansed you from all your shame, and 1 John 1:9 promises that you don't have to carry it any longer: *"If we confess our sins, he is faithful and just and will forgive us our sins and purify us from all unrighteousness"* (NIV). There is no shame in you because there is no shame in Him, and He LIVES in you! It's time to say no to shame.

Shame is the ultimate bully. It chases after you and won't stop until you stop running and make a stand. It's like running from a bully and deciding enough is enough. Now, for those who have heard the words "shame on you" or said to yourself "shame on me," I say, "Shame off you!"

Young leader, in Jesus' name, "Shame off you" right here and right now. Satan be gone now and forever with your lies and accusations. Jesus, I ask you to bring your healing and cleansing; break the power of shame. Amen. *"Therefore, there is now no condemnation for those who are in Christ Jesus"* (Rom. 8:1).

MAKE CRITICISM YOUR FRIEND

As a leader, it is impossible to avoid criticism. If you embrace it, criticism can be your friend and a great teaching tool to help you grow and mature. It's important not to immediately dismiss or get defensive but to be open to finding what might be true. Helpful criticism may also help you see blind spots.

Constructive criticism can be a valuable way to learn from your mistakes. It intends to help you by offering you ways to change and move forward. Destructive criticism, on the other hand, typically comes from a desire to emotionally or spiritually damage you. Constructive criticism is one thing, but fierce criticism is quite another and is harmful. The critical difference is the critics' intention behind their comments.

John Wimber offers some great advice in "Why I Respond to Criticism."[1]

1. *Leaders are to defend their ministries and personal integrity when falsely accused. Jesus did it...the apostles did it, and they instructed other leaders—including us—how to do it.*
2. *Leaders are to take attacks seriously because lies and slander against them and their ministries will hurt, confuse and undermine the faith of those under their care.*
3. *Leaders must publicly acknowledge the truth of accurate criticism and repent in the appropriate biblical manner.*
4. *When a leader is falsely accused in public, they should approach their accuser privately and in the spirit of love, unity, and forgiveness to clarify the issues and be reconciled. If the accuser refuses to respond to a reasonable response, the leader may go forward with their defense.*

As a movement leader, John experienced much criticism. Some justified, some not. One had to do with Vineyard Worship. Vineyard is known for writing and producing fantastic worship songs that are sung all over the world. This criticism was that there were very few songs about the cross. Instead of blowing this off, it got John to thinking and he concluded that there might be some truth to this. So he gathered the various worship songwriters and asked them to begin writing and producing more worship songs about the cross. They responded, and some great and powerful songs about the cross emerged over the next few years.

The lesson here is that although those who criticized John may not have had the best attitude, instead of being defensive, he asked God what He wanted him to learn from this. This became a theme in how John responded to the various criticisms that came his way. "God, what do You want to say to me, and what do You want me to learn from this?" How John did this influenced other leaders like me about how we respond to criticism. It sounds like Joseph: *"You intended to harm me, but God intended it for good"* (Genesis 50:20 NLT).

So, how should you respond to constructive criticism?

- Keep an open mind and, where possible, be willing to own up to your mistakes and try to recover from them.
- If the situation warrants it, always be prepared to apologize.
- Share the criticism with those closest to you and decide if the complaint is justified or not.
- Avoid emotional outbursts or the temptation to respond with criticism to those who criticize you.
- Try not to dwell too much on any criticism you receive. Make plans to act on any changes you need to make and move on.
- Finally, refuse to let bitterness set in and grab your heart!

QUESTIONS FOR THE HEART

1. Is there unforgiveness or bitterness in your life? Explain.

2. Who do you need to forgive? Have you forgiven yourself?

3. Who do you need to ask for forgiveness?

4. How have you had to deal with shame in your life?

5. Is there someone you need to go "the second mile" with and attempt to reconcile?

6. How have you dealt with criticism? Constructively or destructively?

7. Is there someone you need to bless? Do it and watch what happens!

TWELVE
LEAD WITHOUT POWER: TOWEL VS. THE CROWN

HAVE you ever heard the phrase "powering up"? Typically it means using your title, power, or authority to demand compliance or action from those under your authority. It might be something you do with your kids: "I'm the dad, and you will do what I say or else," or "I'm the boss and if you don't do what I say, you're gone!"

This coercive power through threat or force may seem to work on the surface, but in the end, it will eventually come back to bite you in the butt. In an organization, a higher-ranking manager can force a lower-ranking employee to act in a way they don't want to by threatening termination or other disciplinary action. When you resort to this (and sometimes it's inevitable), you lose your ability to lead your people in an equitable fashion. If you continually default to, "Because I say so," it won't be long before you do that in an empty room. I once heard a pastor tell me that he would rather be feared than loved and respected, and his staff responded accordingly. Staff members always knew their job was always on the line, never knowing when the hammer was about to come down. As you would imagine, it was an awful culture with a huge turnover. Few left well. This story, sadly, though common in the marketplace of dog-eat-dog business, also takes place in the church world. Some of the most successful big-time Christian leaders have a legacy of brutality to those they lead. There's got to be a better way—and there is!

You may not like this, but people should not take you too seriously when you first start. Yes, you do have to prove yourself over and over again by pouring your life into those you lead. It takes time to earn spiritual authority or relational authority in people's lives. When I started our church, I had been given positional authority by John Wimber and Tom Stipe to start our church, but I had to earn spiritual authority by leading, caring for and serving the people in Fort Collins.

You only have as much authority in people's lives as they are willing to give you. I love John Maxwell's levels of leadership, and have used them time and again with my leadership training. It is so important to understand the difference between spiritual authority and positional authority if you are going to build strong leaders. I have found four of them especially helpful to me in understanding what authority I have—and don't have—with various people.

The first level is **positional** or title-based authority and realizing that people begin by following you because of your role or position. You are in charge of the ministry someone wants to be a part of, and they are stuck with you. At this level, what you really have is the authority to serve and demonstrate your leadership to them. If they want on the worship team and you are in charge, they follow you because they have no choice. Your shouts are but whispers to them.

Level two is **permission**, or relationship-based. People follow you, not because they have to but because they want to. You have earned their respect. They believe in your leadership and your concern for them as a person. At this level, people give you permission for you to lead them. Balancing your soft and hard side is critical. At this level, your whispers are just beginning to be heard.

Level three is **people development** or empowerment-based.

People follow you because you have invested in their life and helped them go to the next level of leadership. They have become more than they would have been without your investment in their life and ministry. As a result, they give you authority to not only speak into their ministry but also into their personal life. Your whispers have now become shouts to them.

Level four is **personhood** or legacy-based. People now follow you because of who you are, what you represent and how you have lived your life. Your reputation of raising up leaders and your life and ministry is broader and beyond your normal sphere of influence. I have discovered over time that I now actually have a measure of influence on some people that I have never even met. My reputation in raising up young leaders and sending them out is one of the reasons why I have that authority.

When you look at these levels, it is critical to understand that people relate to you in various forms according to their experience or perspective. I had people relating to me at level one and others at the last level. The key for me was to recognize who was at which level and relate to them accordingly. There were times I presumed I had more authority than I actually did and the results were disastrous. One time I took a leap with a couple on staff and spoke into their married life, and the wife was totally offended. I shared stuff that the husband was unwilling to share with her, so I told her what I thought she needed to hear. What I found out immediately was that I did not have that level of authority to speak to her about those things in her life and she blew a gasket and was deeply offended. I did have that level of authority with her husband but not with her. I wish I had known the difference!

This reminds me of something my mentor John Wimber once said: **"I will know if I am your pastor when I have to tell you no!"** I never forgot that. When you have to step up and share hard stuff, you will find out quickly how much authority you actually have or don't have in someone's life.

As a pastor, I learned that for some, I was simply the pastor of our church and to others I was "their" pastor. This is a huge difference that you need to understand. For those for whom I was their pastor, I could speak deeply into their lives, but not so to those who only saw me as the pastor of the church they attended or served in. I had positional authority as to what happened in our church and perhaps in an area they served, but not necessarily in their lives. This was also true for our leaders. Just because someone was a leader did not automatically mean I had earned spiritual authority with them.

Similarly, I was a regional overseer for forty to fifty pastors in my role in the Vineyard movement. For some of those relationships, I was indeed their pastor and had earned that over time. To others, I was only the "Vineyard Rep" and had very little spiritual authority in their lives or churches. I had authority as it pertained to Vineyard issues but nothing more. Every new church that came into our region meant I had to earn the right (spiritual authority) to speak into their lives and church all over again.

ACQUIRING SPIRITUAL AUTHORITY

Jesus used a situation (found in Matthew 20:20-28 NLT) to reinforce how He wanted His disciples to lead (and not to lead) that was totally unlike what they were used to. This is one of the most striking passages from Jesus' teachings on leadership. He first contrasts how the Gentiles (Romans) exercise power and authority versus how it works in His kingdom.

The story begins with James and John's mom coming to Jesus when no one was around with a simple (though outrageous) request. *"In your Kingdom, please let my two sons sit in places of honor next to you, one on your right and the other on your left"* (Matt. 20:21b). Jesus, obviously disturbed, basically tells her that she was out of touch with reality in asking such a thing. He added that it was not His to give anyway, but for His Father who has already prepared those places. As you might imagine, when the disciples got wind of what was going on they were upset. I am not sure if they were only mad at the nerve of this mom and her boys to ask for such a thing, or if maybe they were upset because they got to Jesus first. Then Jesus took the opportunity to set the record straight on His position of authority and how to use it.

But Jesus called them together and said, "You know that the rulers in this world lord it over their people, and officials flaunt their authority over those under them. But among you it will be different. Whoever wants to be a leader among you must be your servant, and whoever wants to be first among you must become your slave. For even the Son of Man came not to be served but to serve others and to give his life as a ransom for many" (Matt. 20:25-28 NIV).

In other words, it might be their way, but it's not My way or yours either! Jesus contrasted what was going on around them but called them to go against the grain of everything they knew and had experienced. Then He gave them the punch line: *"Whoever wants to be a leader among you must be your servant"* (v. 26).

If you want to be a leader that's great, then be humble, be last, sit in the lowest places of honor, and become like a child. This had to be a stunning moment for the disciples, as it was totally opposite how leaders acted around them. I find it interesting that the term *leader* is mentioned only a handful of times in the New Testament whereas the term *servant* is mentioned over 900 times. Get it? Worship leader? When was the last time you volunteered to lead in kids ministry or sing over the babies in the nursery? Pastor? When was the last time you cleaned the restrooms, mopped the floor, or spent a Sunday teaching the third graders? It's so easy for us to forget where we came from. Sometimes we serve to get where we want to be and then assume another posture when we get there.

JESUS IS OUR SUPREME EXAMPLE

In Philippians 2:3-4, Paul writes, *"Don't be selfish; don't try to impress others. Be humble, thinking of others as better than yourselves. Don't look out only for your own interests, but take an interest in others, too"* (NLT). Paul is not pulling any punches here, telling us that leadership is not about me or you! It's about Jesus and those whom we serve, not what we get, nor how many people follow us, nor anything else. You know what's interesting? When someone does not have long to live, you know what is most important to them. And what Paul chose to write about was what was most important to him as he was writing from a Roman prison, knowing his time was short.

Then the apostle Paul presents Jesus as the ultimate example of what it means to be a servant (leader) in Philippians 2:5-11:

> *You **must** have the same attitude that Christ Jesus had. Though he was God, he did not think of equality with God as something to cling to. Instead, he gave up his divine privileges; he took the humble position of a slave and was born as a human being. When he appeared in human form, he humbled himself in obedience to God and died a criminal's death on a cross. Therefore, God elevated him to the place of highest honor and gave him the name above all other names, that at the name of Jesus every knee should bow, in heaven and on earth and under the earth, and every tongue declares that Jesus Christ is Lord, to the glory of God the Father.*

There's so much to unpack here! Paul says that having the same attitude as Jesus is not optional. Giving up our rights and privileges is part of the deal. Jesus chose to deny Himself His rightly deserved divine privileges and took the humble position of a slave. In contrast, some popular Christian leaders today often flaunt all the privileges they have from being "successful" in growing large ministries. They have entourages, limousines, jets, and every other unimaginable luxuries. King Solomon had everything a man could want and ended up feeling it was all in vain. (Read Ecclesiastes 1:14.)

In Fort Collins, as our church grew quite large, there were times I had to fight off this attitude of entitlement. People would tell me I needed a larger salary, a bigger house, a nicer car, clothes, etc. Rick Warren was and is a great example to me as he drives an older car, lives in the same house, does not have a jet, and has kept a modest standard of living. Being the pastor of one of the largest and most influential churches in America, he could have easily felt justified having anything he wanted. But he was content with what he had and his success never went to his head. I believe contentment is a lost virtue these days that we need to recapture. Thank you Rick for your example! Jesus didn't just talk about servanthood; He lived it and demonstrated it over and over again.

BRING BACK THE TOWEL

In the upper room for the last supper, Jesus had one last opportunity for His disciples to understand what it meant to be a servant leader because they still were not getting this servant thing. In John 13, is the infamous story of Jesus washing the feet of His disciples, which illustrates the reality of God's upside down kingdom.

In *Faithmapping: A Gospel Atlas for Your Spiritual Journey*, Daniel Montgomery and Mike Cosper write about the custom of washing one another's feet:

> Footwashing was a common practice in Jesus's day. Roads were just dirt, and people would have worn sandals of rope and leather. Combine the sweat-inducing heat with nearly bare feet and dusty roads, and you can imagine the result. When you entered a home it was common courtesy to have a servant wash your feet. It was customary at the end of the day for a Rabbi's disciples when they arrived for the evening meal to wash their hands and feet and then those who came after them.

When Jesus washed the disciples' feet (recorded in John 13:1-17), it appeared that something wasn't right. He was the guest of honor and yet no one had washed His feet. Not even His disciples considered their master's dignity and comfort at the meal. So as they bickered about their roles in the coming kingdom, He got up, disrobed, assumed the role of a slave, and began washing their feet. Jesus, what are you doing? Messiahs don't wash feet—or do they?

THE LESSON OF THE TOWEL

This is a pivotal moment, so much so that Jesus finally gives up on words. He had told them numerous parables about being a servant. Now He will perform the most humiliating role for someone of his stature, the washing of feet, leaving the disciples speechless. Jesus, who has power and authority over everything on earth, is now crawling on His hands and knees among a bunch of filthy feet!

Peter can't handle it and declares, *"No, you shall never wash my feet"* (John 13:8 NIV). What Peter meant was, "Jesus is too good to wash my feet. It's the job of a slave not of a Rabbi and certainly not the Messiah!" I love how the New Living Translation interprets Jesus's response to Peter, also in verse 8: Unless I wash you, you won't belong to me." Then Peter goes all in with "not just my feet but my hands and my head as well!" (John 13:9 NIV). Don't you just love Peter's all-or-nothing attitude?

THE WAY UP IS DOWN

But this moment isn't about Peter; it's about Jesus, demonstrating to the disciples (and to all of history) that the greatest among us is the one who serves out of a love that overflows from the heart. As Jesus gets on His hands and knees to scrub the filthy feet of His disciples, He is essentially saying, "The way up is down, and greatness is not about being served but serving others."

Then the big moment comes as Jesus asks them this question: *"Do you understand what I have done for you?"* (John 13:12 NIV).

I can imagine the disciples shaking their heads yes and no at the same time. Jesus continues, *"You call me 'Teacher' and 'Lord' and rightly so, for that is what I am"* (John 13:13 NIV). I think Jesus wants them not to misunderstand: Just because He washed their feet didn't mean that He was less than they thought He was.

And next comes the climax! *"Now that I, your Lord and Teacher, have washed your feet you also should wash one another's feet"* (John 13:15 NIV). I can just picture Peter reaching for his bucket because he knows what's coming. "Now that I have washed your feet,......... you should now wash 'my feet'" Of course, who wouldn't jump up to wash Jesus's feet, but that's not how it went down. Instead Jesus continues, "You should wash each other's feet."

"No, Jesus, I want to wash your feet, not Nathaniel's! Have you seen his feet? Come on, you can't be serious?" The big point here is that we all say we want to serve Jesus, but He says, "The way you serve Me is by serving others." He closes by saying, *"Now that you know these things, you will be blessed **if you do them**"* (v. 17).

Coming into Jerusalem, the people wanted to crown Jesus King of the Jews, but He would have none of it. Too often it seems like some of us are looking for the crown rather than the towel. The Bible talks about a crown we will receive in the next life but the only one we get here is the one Jesus got—a crown of thorns. So if you want a crown, I guess you can have that one. If Jesus took up the towel, don't you think we should too? It's amazing how much more people listen to us when we are looking up (not down) as we are washing their feet and serving them. Jesus never talked down to people and left us a great example to follow. Another takeaway here is to remember that regardless of any title or position you attain, there is nothing that is beneath you or me that we should be unwilling to do.

I remember a time when we were hosting a major conference on God's heart for the poor in Fort Collins. Pastors came from around the world to participate in our gathering. We had scheduled various kinds of outreaches in the city, including cleaning toilets, passing out sunscreen, cleaning windshields, and car washes, etc. One pastor, who was the leader of a major European denomination, actually refused to go on the outreaches, as he saw it beneath him, especially the toilet cleaning crew that Steve Sjogren and I led. If Jesus can wash dirty feet, there is no task that is beneath any of us.

GIVING YOUR LIFE AWAY

Have you discovered that you are most alive when you are serving others? As it was with Jesus, so it is with you and me. If Jesus was the God of the towel, then we should be the people of the towel. When I teach this, I close by having multiple stacks of small wash cloths with a crown on top of them. I then challenge attendees to come up and lift up the crown (reject it) and take a towel, and put it in a place where it will remind them of being the servant they are supposed to be. I know some worship leaders who put it in their guitar case or piano, others in their Bible or office desk. I keep mine in my car where I need to be reminded that I am not the "king of the road."

Do you prefer being closer to the throne, nearer the people of power and the place of privilege? I hope not. Beginning to end, Jesus embraced His mission with the towel, seeking the lost, performing miracles, healing the lepers and those in the margins, casting out demons, loving people, praying, fasting, and doing many other acts of service to humanity. The values of God's kingdom are different from the values of this world. In the world, greatness is judged by the power a person exercises over others. In the kingdom of God, greatness is judged by service to people. If someone tries to crown you, run the other way as fast as you can.

LEADING WITHOUT POWER ON DISPLAY

A great example of God's upside down kingdom is Dr. Luis Bush, an icon in the global missions movement. He leads a powerful global ministry called Trans World Mission, and also led the missional 10-40 Window Movement which is the geographical window of the most unreached people groups on earth. He later helped launch what is now known as the 4/14 Window Movement, which Becky and I now lead. The 4/14 movement is based on the fact that most people who come into relationship with Jesus do so between the ages of 4 and 14. George Barna, among others, has substantiated this in surveys and studies over the years. Bush's whispers have become God's shouts to me as he embodies and personifies what leading without power looks like. Two events demonstrate and shaped how Luis moved from having positional authority to spiritual authority in my life.

My first encounter with Luis Bush was at a 4/14 Global Summit in Singapore 2011 with attendees from 92 countries. He shared during the first session, and I was captured from the beginning by his passion. I heard him say, "God is raising up a generation to change the world. We will do this by reaching, rescuing, rooting and releasing them as full partners in God's mission." By the end of the summit, I was all in and ready to give the rest of my life to this vision.

But something else happened during the last session that left a lasting impression on my life. The teenagers took the stage. They led worship and shared some stories, but due to a few scheduling issues, some of the plans for the younger teens to participate were cut out of the planned program. One of the key teen leaders took offense and went ballistic on stage as he took the mic and proceeded to scold the leaders and audience for the decision; he went on and on with his tirade. As I watched this unfold, I wondered what Luis and the other leaders were going to do. In this culture, what this teen did would have been considered incredibly shameful and dishonoring. I thought to myself, "When is somebody going to grab that mic and get this guy off the stage? He is ruining the end of this Global Summit!"

Then, to my complete shock and amazement, I watched Luis in front of a thousand mission leaders from around the world, go up to the young man, fall to the floor on his knees, and ask for his forgiveness. The place went silent. Sadly, the teenager went on a while longer, but Luis stayed right there on his knees until he put the mic down and walked away. Then Luis got up, put his arm around the teen, and publicly repented to the group for curtailing some of the planned programs for the young people. Instead of publicly rebuking the teen, Luis prayed for him and all the teenagers in the room. I walked away with a deep appreciation of a servant leader who humbled himself in front of his peers and refused to use his power to crush this young man who was clearly out of line. I said to myself, "I can follow a man like that." Little did I know at the time that was exactly what God had in store for me.

The second event occurred during a World Prayer Assembly in Jakarta with thousands attending from all over the world. Luis Bush was one of the keynote speakers at the end of the conference, but speaker after speaker went over their time allotment, which created a dilemma. Either someone does not get to speak or the conference goes longer, and many people have to leave to catch their flights home. There was a female pastor from Africa who was due to speak before Luis, but they were already way over the time and there was no way Luis was not going to find a way for her to speak. Luis decided that she was more important than he was. He gave up his keynote speaking moment to her. Wow, so many speakers were selfish and careless with their time, and Luis gave up his teaching slot because of it. For Luis, none of that event was about him, so it really wasn't that unreasonable to defer to the African speaker.

After this incident, I progressed from "I can follow a man like that" to "I want to be a leader like Luis Bush." He had—and still has—level four authority in my life. I have never seen a man of his stature do what he did in these two instances. Everywhere Luis goes, he presents himself only as a servant of Jesus, nothing more or less. That is his only posture. Not only does it serve him well, but it is also a huge example to me and others who follow him. Titles mean little to Luis, and yet he carries immense spiritual authority everywhere he goes. When Luis knelt before that teenage boy in Singapore, it reminded me of Jesus kneeling before His disciples as He washed their feet. That's what Luis Bush did that day; he metaphorically took out his bucket and washed the feet of that teenage boy in Singapore. As a result, what began as whispers have become shouts to me and so many others.

To lead without power is to understand spiritual authority and how it works. All authority is given by God but earned in the lives of the people we serve. It is not automatic. The difference between spiritual authority and positional authority is expansive, and if you don't know the difference, you are in for a big struggle. As you grow in your spiritual authority, you move from your shouts being whispers to your whispers becoming shouts.

QUESTIONS FOR THE HEART

1, How have you responded when someone "powered up" on you?

2. Do you lead from spiritual or positional authority? Be honest.

3. Are your whispers shouts or are your shouts whispers? Explain.

4. How do you earn spiritual authority?

5. Do you feel the need to control people? Why?

6. Do people feel empowered or held back by your leadership?

7. List leaders who have authority in your life at the various levels one through four described in this chapter. Then list people whose lives you have authority in at those same levels.

THIRTEEN
MAKE SURE OF YOUR CALLING

According to George Barna, "Vision is a clear mental portrait of a preferable future, communicated by God to His chosen servant-leaders, based upon an accurate understanding of God, self and circumstances." True vision comes from God and not one from your own making. If you want to be a leader, vision is not optional.

You need to have a direction, a vision, purpose and yes, a calling. Zig Ziglar put it this way, "If you aim at nothing, you will hit it every time." Your calling is not a "whatever" deal. I know it is a popular expression today but a "whatever" attitude takes you anywhere and nowhere as you go in and out with the tides. We are not called to live a "whatever" life. Without a vision, leaders tend to lead people to themselves which is the worst case scenario.

Not having a vision or goal is like shooting a basketball without a goal/net! You need a vision from God, not something you pull out of a hat! It's having a deep sense of where you are, what you are doing and where you are going, that God is leading the way.

The apostle Paul did not have a "whatever" attitude like many do today. He had a sense of purpose and destiny. He saw all of life as a training event to accomplish what God called Him to do. I love the fact that Paul likened his life and ministry to competing as a runner, not running aimlessly but running to win. Consider what he wrote in 1 Corinthians 9:24-27:

> *Don't you realize that in a race everyone runs, but only one person gets the prize? So run to win! All athletes are disciplined in their training. They do it to win a prize that will fade away, but we do it for an eternal prize. So I run with purpose in every step. I am not just shadow boxing. I discipline my body like an athlete, training it to do what it should. Otherwise, I fear that after preaching to others I myself might be disqualified* (NLT).

BE IN IT TO WIN IT

Paul says, "Run to win." I like that. It's not running just to run. In my football coaching days, I knew that some coaches played with a "not to lose" attitude rather than a "whatever it takes" to win. It is a mindset, and it makes a big difference. When you know what the game is and what's on the line, you do whatever it takes to accomplish the goal. How many times have you seen your favorite team lose at the end of a game because they became really conservative and started to play it safe? I loved it when a team played "prevent defense" against us because it usually meant we were probably going to score. Playing to win is much better than playing not to lose. Jesus did not give His life for you or me to lose, but so we could make it to His winner's circle. It is an attitude, but it is also a discipline. (And if you read to the end of the book, spoiler alert: we win!)

But ... you can't win if you are trying to run somebody else's race. And you won't win if you don't stay focused. I have learned this the hard way. In leading our church in Colorado, sometimes I tried to do other people's jobs at the expense of my own and struggled at times to stay in my lane. For instance, I would rearrange the chairs in the auditorium, replace lightbulbs in the lobby, insert myself in our communications, social media and video teams, and try to solve staff issues that were other people's responsibilities. My advice to you is let those you lead do their job and you do yours!

Paul was acutely aware of the possibility that he might somehow be disqualified, which is why he talked about the need for discipline and staying focused on the prize. He was not about running aimlessly without a purpose. You need to believe that where you are at, and what you are doing, is where you are supposed to be. If you are in school then be all in with school and get all you can out of it. Be all in no matter what season you are in and whatever you are doing. Single? Be all in! Working at 7/11? Be all in! Married? Kids? Be all in! Working or leading in the marketplace? Be all in! Pastoring a church? Be all in! Get it?

Having a "whatever" attitude accomplishes nothing and gets us on an endless treadmill and ultimately leaves us alone in a sea of regret. Don't go there because God has uniquely put something in you, and He will get it done in your life if you let Him. Paul said it best to the Colossians, and it is especially good for those of you who lead in the marketplace. *"Work willingly at whatever you do, as though you were working for the Lord rather than for people. Remember that the Lord will give you an inheritance as your reward, and that the Master you are serving is Christ"* (Col. 3:23 NLT).

Paul gives us an insider's look at his calling in his letter to the Galatians. He discovered that his purpose and calling was to give his life to reaching out to the Gentiles (non-Jewish people) so they too may know Christ. He lived the rest of his life 24/7 for that very purpose. Finding his purpose was a journey of discovery, but at some point he realized his calling and stayed in this lane for the rest of his life. Consider what Paul wrote in Galatians 1:15-16: *"But **even before I was born, God chose me** and called me by his marvelous grace. Then it pleased him to reveal his Son to me so* that I would **proclaim the Good News about Jesus** to the Gentiles" (NLT emphasis added).

WHAT IF YOU HAVE NO VISION?

What do you do if you don't know your purpose and don't have a specific vision for your life? You can serve someone else's vision until God gives you your own. I see this in Scripture and in life. Your calling might actually be to serve someone else's vision for the rest of your life. When I think of Jonathan and David's relationship, Jonathan's purpose was to serve and protect David from his father who sought to take his life. Without Jonathan, David probably doesn't make it. Some of us are called to be Davids, and others are called to a Jonathan or a Barnabas. Sometimes your calling is actually serving someone else's vision!

The road to finding your personal purpose often begins by serving someone else's vision. Much of what I have achieved began this way. When I first began going to Amman, Jordan, I did not have a vision for Arabs or the Middle East, but I met a man who did. His name was Afeef Halasah, and for the next twenty-two years I hooked my wagon up to his and served his vision (AFTA, Arabs for the Arabs). As a result, I began assisting Afeef in coaching and training Christian and Muslim background believers and pastors. He eventually invited us to start an English-speaking church in Amman. It has been an incredible run, and God has opened so many doors for me by serving Afeef's vision for the Arab world.

Similarly, in the late 80s through the 90s, God called me to serve YWAM Austria leader Bruce Clewett, who became a lifelong friend. His vision was to reach out and train young Catholic leaders while establishing "small communities of faith" within the Catholic church world. I spoke and brought teams to several conferences, seminars, and training events with mostly Catholics in attendance. It was so powerful and rewarding—and fruitful. At one point we brought nearly a hundred people with us from around the U.S. and sent them to various cities in Central Europe as the Communist Iron Curtain was coming down. Over a five-year period of time, we sent over four hundred people on ministry teams there, and it all started with serving the vision of Bruce Clewett.

Bruce is a great example of what it means to wait for God to raise you up. ***If God doesn't give it to you, you don't want it***. Let God raise you up. You don't have to strive to get what God has for you. Obedience and faithfulness is the doorway to whatever future God has for you. You don't have to chase after ministry or positions. Bruce's story of coming to Austria via Germany and the U.S. is quite fascinating and helpful for understanding that serving another man's vision prepares you for the future God has in store for you. Some of the most fruitful times I have experienced in my ministry have come from doing this. I think it's healthy to serve outside the confines of your ministry context, which is why I was a volunteer chaplain for the Fort Collins Police Department for over twenty years.

Bruce's Story

One day I heard a voice inside my head say, "I am calling you to go to Austria. But first, you are to return to Germany and continue serving Keith Warrington (my Youth With A Mission leader at the time."

After the demonstration, I made my way back to YWAM's Hurlach Castle in southern Germany to join Keith and his team. I was fully expecting that this would be a temporary assignment after which I would move on to the country where my "real" ministry would begin.

I was so wrong! Five years passed before I left Germany to launch a YWAM ministry in Austria. In retrospect, those five years proved to be a critical part of God's preparation for my role as the national YWAM leader of Austria. I discovered that by serving another person's vision, I was able to learn lessons and hone skills which would later be vital for me as the leader of a national ministry.

I also realized that I needed to "plant roots" in Germany if I was going to bear any fruit for God's kingdom in either Germany or Austria. So, I made a conscious effort to develop deep emotional, spiritual, ministry and social ties to Germany and its people. (I even married a German gal!) When I finally did leave, it was kind of like transplanting a sapling from Germany to Austria rather than simply starting with only a seed. The result was that our team was fruitful right from the start in Austria.

Additionally, I am so glad for the character-building lessons God allowed me to learn in Germany before launching out on this adventure in Austria.

I once heard someone say, "The higher the building, the deeper the foundation. People see the buildings, but the foundations are built below the surface, out of the public eye."

When God gives you an awesome vision, be ready for Him to do a lot of foundation-building in your life – especially in the area of character. God desires for you to not only do great things for Him, but also to become transformed into the likeness of His Son. And that is a lifelong process. (2 Corinthians 3:18)

I encourage you to invest yourself wholeheartedly into the people and place where He has put you for now. Be eager to learn all that He wants to teach you there before He moves you on to the next thing He has for you.

Bruce Clewett, YWAM Austria

A LOST OPPORTUNITY ... OR NOT THE RIGHT TIME?

When I was 25, a pastor flew down to where I was and offered me an incredible youth pastor position at a huge church in San Francisco. I somehow said no to this amazing opportunity with a good salary (which I could have really used), but it wasn't the right time as I had my teenage brothers living with me. I felt it would be wrong to uproot them and go and take this job. Looking back, I have no regrets because it was the right thing to do. When God was ready, He called me to Colorado, and I have achieved far more than I could have imagined. But I needed to wait on God, and I realized that my brothers actually helped me wait and not jump until it was God's time to move on. Soon after they graduated from high school and had left the house, I met my future wife, Becky. We were married, and a couple of years later we moved to Colorado. Nothing was wasted; it was all part of God's plan for my life. If I had jumped at all the opportunities I had when I was 23, it could have short-circuited God's ultimate plan for me.

Sure, you can try and make ministry happen, but even if you get what you worked for, you can feel illegitimate. Did God do this, or did I manipulate the circumstances to make it happen? King Saul felt threatened by young David, but David had no aspiration to take anything from Saul let alone his throne. However, Saul refused to be consoled. He lived in constant fear and jealousy of David. David could have tried to make it happen, but he chose to wait for God's timing for him to be king. And later, David indeed did become king and to this day is revered as the greatest king in the history of Israel. If God didn't give him the throne, David didn't want it. This is why he refused to undermine or kill Saul when he had the chance. Remember what people were saying after Saul and David came home from the battle against Goliath and the Philistines? "And the women sang one to another as they played, and said, Saul hath slain his thousands, and David his ten thousands" (1 Sam. 18:7 ASV). David didn't take the bait but would wait his time.

In Luke 14, Jesus tells a very powerful story about humility and waiting on God. Jesus was at the home of a Pharisee and noticed how the guests picked the places of honor at the table which opened the door for Him to share a powerful lesson. Jesus told them that when you are invited to a big party, do not take the place of honor or someone more important than you may show up and the host comes and gives your place to them. Instead, when you get invited to some big party or banquet, take the least important place at the table so that this time the host will come and say that they have a better place for you. Then you will be honored rather than embarrassed before all. Then the clincher comes in Luke 14:11: *"For all of those who exalt themselves will be humbled and those who humble themselves will be exalted"* (NIV). What a good picture of what it means to wait on God and trust Him with your future. God is the host and He will decide when, where, and how you will find your place in life. Entitlement and self-promotion are ugly traits, especially in those of us who follow Jesus.

Sometimes we don't want to wait for God, and we offer all kinds of excuses why we couldn't wait. A great case in point is a time when Saul was leading his troops against the Philistines and was waiting at Gilgal for Samuel to come and offer appropriate sacrifices. After seven days, Saul refused to wait any longer, and he took matters into his own hands and offered the sacrifice himself. (1 Samuel 13:7-14) Just as Samuel was finishing the burnt offerings Samuel showed up. He actually called Saul "foolish" and said, *"You have not kept the command the Lord your God gave you"* (1 Sam. 13:13). Saul, like we often do, offered all kinds of excuses for his decision. But as a result, Samuel declared that Saul's kingdom would end. God had found a man after his own heart and appointed David to be the leader of His people. Not waiting for God was the beginning of the end for Saul and is a great lesson for us to learn.

HOW PRIDE DESTROYS LIVES

First Peter 5:6 says, *"Humble yourself therefore, under God's mighty hand, that he may lift you up in due time"* (NIV). Pride pushes you to seek places you think you deserve rather than where God has chosen you to serve. Serving another person's vision is hard to do when pride takes hold of you. Being humble and waiting is part of a servant leader's lifestyle. It means learning and growing through disappointments and trials. Don't chafe under the Lord's discipline; it means He loves you and wants the best for you. Peter goes on to say, *"Give all your worries and cares to God for he cares all about you"* (1 Pet. 5:7 NLT). It really comes down to trusting God with your future. Remember **nobody can stop God's will from happening in your life…except you!** And the path of God's call seldom goes in a straight line.

David Brooks' Story

Child labor, poverty and an extremely emotionally and physically abusive father were a part of my story from childhood until I was thirteen years old when Child Protective Services took my siblings and me away from that painful reality. Trying to fill an emptiness inside, I turned to drugs and alcohol and the wrong crowd. But at sixteen years old, I gave my life to Christ because of the investment of a youth pastor, Darryl Castillo, who took a special interest in me and believed God had a special plan for my life. He nurtured my faith. I met him when my two eldest brothers convinced me to go to church for the first time. As time went on, Pastor Darryl would continually put his hand on my shoulder and say, "God has a plan for you." So, even though I was young in my faith, I jumped right into ministry in my high school and college years. And then later, I had an invitation to be on staff at a church as one of the pastors.

I never found out why but I never got that job; instead, for three years I served as a full-time volunteer intern at that church. Maybe I was immature or had some character flaw or maybe it was not God's timing. After experiencing frustration, heartbreak and broken promises connected to what I thought was "God's plan," I found myself angry at God and disconnected from community. In my hurt, I ran from God and found myself in Colorado in a MA social worker program at Colorado State

University. I was deeply dissatisfied and some of my destructive life style choices left me empty, broken and at a low point in my life.

I had experienced so much of Jesus' goodness and favor in my early years of following Christ, including successful ministry. But in my bitterness and anger, I found myself living a life that was inconsistent with the love and transformation I had experienced in Jesus. I needed freedom from my bitterness and to let God heal things in me that went all the way back to my abusive father. Forgiving him opened a door for all that has happened to me since that time.

I ended up at the Vineyard Church of the Rockies in Fort Collins, Colorado, where God used the pastors and community to love me back to life. When I showed up at the church that first Sunday, Pastor Ricko (what we called him) was giving a talk on generosity and serving our community...my cynicism thought, "Here we go, another pastor asking for money." But at the end of his message, he didn't ask for money. Instead, something incredible happened. He said, "One of the greatest needs of those who are homeless in our city is not having good shoes. So often we give what we don't need any more—but not usually our best stuff. You are probably wearing your best shoes right now, and I am asking you to leave them under your chairs and we will give them away to the homeless." I thought to myself, "This is crazy; who's going to leave their Sunday best shoes?" But to my amazement, more than seventy-five percent of the church walked to their cars shoeless. I was amazed and said, "This is the kind of church I want to be a part of, a group of people that selflessly meets the needs of others, a church that not only talks about it but does it." Later someone called it "sharing God's love in practical ways."

I finished my master's degree, started volunteering at the church and became an intern and then a staff pastor. God's plan for my life was coming into view. In my ten years there, under Rick Olmstead's leadership, I learned about my true identity, the Father heart of God and what it means to truly walk in step with *the Holy Spirit. I also learned about humility, the concept of "growing where God has planted you and a healthy culture of honor," among many other amazing life lessons.*

Hindsight is an amazing gift. If I could share one nugget of wisdom to my younger self or even with someone who is just starting out on their journey of discovering God's plan and purpose for their lives, I would say this. Even when you can't see it, God has a plan for your life! If you trust Him, walk in forgiveness and surrender your life to His leading, He will guide you through every season and every storm in surprising ways. God is more interested in enjoying time with you than what you can do for Him. Invest in your character formed by daily time in God's Word and presence rather than depending on your natural talents and spiritual giftings.

David Brooks, Father, husband and church planter in waiting

Isaiah 40:31 says, *"But those who wait on the Lord shall renew their strength; They shall mount up with wings like eagles, They shall run and not be weary, They shall walk and not faint"* (NKJV).

Wait for God to raise you up because he is more than capable. I have met a number of frustrated leaders who feel unappreciated and left out. God is able to move you where He wants you to be. He may remove the leader whom you feel is holding you back, but don't have anything to do with the leader being removed. It will leave a bad taste in your mouth.

BEWARE OF HIJACKERS

But be careful as there will be those who may want to use your church or ministry to promote their vision or agenda and hijack yours. This is why it's essential that you know what your purpose and vision is. If you don't, there will be plenty of visions coming toward you from every which way. I am not saying not to address the hard and important issues of our day, but do it in a thoughtful, loving, biblical and Jesus-honoring way. Refuse to let seasonal political winds drive you off course. Satan is always at work to hijack the mission of Jesus. I have seen too many churches derailed because their leaders allowed the political arena to drive and overtake the mission of the church.

I encourage you to stay apolitical as much as possible realizing Jesus deeply loves those on both sides of the aisle or those who have no aisle at all. Political issues and powerful personalities have divided us long enough. The "God is on our side" rhetoric has caused so much harm in the name of the Christian faith. History is full of examples of this including the Crusades, Inquisitions, Northern Ireland, and so much more, all in the name of "God is on our side," which some used to justify doing horrific things in the name of Jesus. I think Jesus' words, *"Depart from me I never knew you" might come into play here.* (Matthew 7:23)

TURNING VISION INTO REALITY

I love the story of Nehemiah as he goes from a simple cupbearer to the King of Persia to the restorer and builder of the gates and walls of Jerusalem. Who would have thought that this obscure figure would even consider such an outlandish pursuit? But Nehemiah dared to believe God and stepped out into an impossible dream that became reality. Young leaders, as we walk through the steps Nehemiah went through, I hope it can inspire you and give you a framework of how vision is born, developed and executed. Whether in the marketplace or a church setting, the principles found here are fundamental for every leader's pursuit of vision.

1. Vision is born in the heart. (Compassion) Nehemiah's vision began when news came to him from one of his brothers about the devastation in Jerusalem where the walls had been torn down and the gates destroyed. Something landed deep in Nehemiah's heart that caused him to agonize over the plight of those there. He could have easily had the attitude of "why should I care? It's's not my problem and what can I do anyway? I am a lowly cupbearer to the king. I drink what is intended for the king in case it's poisoned. If it is, the king lives and they need to find another cupbearer." But God made it Nehemiah's problem. Vision is first and foremost born in the heart, and it doesn't go away until you respond. Teddy Roosevelt famously said, "People don't care how much you know until they know how much you care."

2. Prayer and fasting (Intercession). When Nehemiah heard about the devastation in Jerusalem, he sat down and wept, as he prayed and fasted for days. He could not get over what he was feeling because God put it there. Day and night he cried out to the Lord for the plight of those in Jerusalem. Nehemiah was unwilling to stop until he heard from the Lord on what he was to do. Too many times we ask God to bless our plans rather than waiting for His.

3. Faith and a plan of action (Strategy). Then somewhere along the line God gave him his assignment (vision) and a plan of what to do, including going to the king and asking him for what he needed. From a broken heart, to prayer and fasting, faith is born as God's vision comes into view. So it started with compassion, weeping, prayer, faith, strategy and then it was time for action.

4. Off to see the king (Action). So Nehemiah got off his knees and at great risk, he went before the king with the plan. Nehemiah didn't go right away but waited until the next spring when the time would be just right. Young leader, too often we get so excited about our vision that we get ahead of God and we prematurely barrel full steam ahead. It is one thing to have a vision of what God has for you to do but quite another to step out in God's timing. As he approached the king, he could not hide his deeply troubled heart as he unloaded all he was feeling about the plight of Jerusalem. And low and behold the king said, "Okay, what do you need?" What a great moment! But can you imagine if Nehemiah had no plan at this point? "Well, um, I, um, didn't think I would get this far and was not sure my head would still be on my shoulders, so let me get back to you on that." (For a cupbearer to be sad in the king's presence usually meant your head was headed for the platter.)

5. Onward to Jerusalem! (Incarnation). Nehemiah next loaded up all the provisions provided by the king and took off for Jerusalem. The first thing he did before meeting with any of the city leaders was prayer-walk the streets to see for himself the devastation he had heard about. There was no display or bravado of "no fear Nehemiah's here"! He did not present himself as some hero coming on a white horse (or camel). Night after night he ventured out as God broke his heart even more as Nehemiah thought about what to do next. I mentioned that we have helped launch well over 30 churches and in each case I implored every church planter to start by walking the streets of their city and get God's heart before they launch anything. If you don't get His heart for where you are going you need to find another city to serve and love.

6. Nehemiah meets with city leaders (Honor). Finally, Nehemiah gathered the priests, nobles, and the officials and declared, "You see the trouble we are in. Jerusalem lies in ruins and its gates have been burned"—and I love this next part— *"Come, let's rebuild Jerusalem's wall, so that we will no longer be a disgrace"* (Neh. 2:17 Christian Standard Bible).

Nehemiah identifies himself as one of them (trouble "we" are in) and gives them a picture of not just what was wrong, but what could be. He gave them a different picture of the future of Jerusalem. It's so easy to focus on what's wrong rather than what is possible, which is why sometimes we need a Nehemiah to come to town and awaken us to the plans God has in store for us. He did not dishonor the leaders who did not need a lecture of all that is wrong but a plan and vision to make things right. Nehemiah gave them God's vision and...they said *yes*, let's do it! It's so easy for us to get used to the darkness and devastation in our lives. The officials had gotten used to life in Jerusalem.

"It's just the way it is around here." Yet one man comes to town with a vision and a plan and they respond, "Why not? Let's do it!" Now that is the power of vision, my friend, and it's so much better than any of our best ideas of how to motivate and activate people. When you show people what is possible, they just might do it!

For a number of years, I took our staff pastors to the Global Leadership Summit sponsored by Willow Creek Association, but I grew weary after a while and somewhat frustrated trying to come up with our next BHAG (The Big Hairy Audacious Goal, which is something only God can do). In 2010, out of some real soul searching, I began crying out to God saying, "Lord, I am so tired of our best ideas and BHAGs. I need You to speak to us about what You want us to do."

Not long after that, my wife Becky received an invitation to the 2011 Global 4/14 Window Movement Summit in Singapore. It was a conference about awakening a generation to change the world. Becky did not want me to go because she thought I would be a distraction since it was about kids, which was not my forte for sure. Anyway, after much prodding I convinced her to get me an invite, so we went and—surprise, surprise—God had a life-changing encounter in store for me.

Toward the end of the summit, I had a powerful Holy Spirit moment as God grabbed and awakened my heart for this young generation. I then heard God say to me, "I want you to give the rest of your life to this and your life is about to make sense." I was not sure exactly what that meant. Give my life to this movement or to raising up the next generation? (It turned out to be both as eight years later, Becky and I were chosen to lead the 4/14 Movement.) As I arrived home following that Singapore conference, I was asked by the national director of the Vineyard to lead the youth and young adult task forces which confirmed what I had heard in Singapore. I also knew that God wanted our church to become focused on the young generation, which we did. At one point we had over four hundred young adults gathered on Sunday nights, and our kids and youth ministries were thriving. Yes, it was still a BHAG but one that came from God this time, and was so much more fun because God was obviously leading the way.

7. Mobilizing the workers (The Work Begins). It's one thing for the leaders to vote *yes* on a vision, but if the people vote *no*, the vision dies right there. Nehemiah not only recruited the leaders of the city, but now he went with the leaders to the people. What would they say? Incredibly, they said *yes*, and people all over the city came forward offering their various skills and resources to begin the work of restoring the walls and gates of the city. It must have been quite the sight to behold. It's interesting that Nehemiah 3 records all these obscure people with hard-to-pronounce names. It might be easy to jump right over chapter 3 as mundane, but without the people saying *yes*, no walls or gates would have been restored and the book of Nehemiah would never have been written. What a great lesson to learn about getting buy-in for the vision and not just from the leaders, but also from those who will do the work and make it happen.

8. So, I prayed (Dealing with Opposition). As the work progressed, so did the opposition from their enemies who ridiculed them and threatened to attack them to stop the work. Nehemiah's response was to call the people to prayer, remember the Lord, and stand their ground. Nehemiah was not away in an ivory tower that some leaders retreat to in times of trouble. He was right there with them on the front lines. The vision was so embedded in Nehemiah that there was no way he was going to back off now. That's what visionary leaders do. In hard times when we are challenged, we need leaders like Nehemiah who will remind us what God has said and will not abandon us when the battle gets hard.

9. Mid-course correction (Be Flexible). It's critical for a leader to continue to seek the Lord every step of the way, not just at the beginning. There was not a "No, God I can take it from here" attitude. Nehemiah demonstrated his dependence on God every step of the way. Nehemiah shifted his strategy and put guards behind the most vulnerable parts of the wall construction with half working while the other half stood guard. He also had to deal with dissension and some injustices that emerged among the people. He was a hands-on leader. Like Nehemiah and every successful leader, you will have to make mid-course corrections along the way. If you have a boat and pick a point on the other side and don't adjust, you will not end up where you wanted to.

10. Refuse to get distracted (Keep Your Eyes on the Prize). Distractions work against us like nothing else does. It is so easy to get distracted from what God has called us to do. Our enemy, the devil, is relentless and works around the clock to get us off vision. As the work continued toward completion, Nehemiah's enemies took more shots at stopping the work. They'd sent a message to Nehemiah to meet in the plain of Ono. (If you get a message like that, your response needs to be "Oh, no, I won't go!") What a play on words. Nehemiah refused to take the bait and refused to stop the work. I love his reply, *"I am engaged in a great work, so I can't come. Why should I stop working to come and meet with you?"* (Neh. 6:3 NLT). This is what a vision from God does. You know what you are for and what God has given you to do, and nothing will stop or distract you from it! I love Nehemiah's response to his enemies whose final plot was to sow false accusations that he and the Jews are preparing to rebel against the king, and directly threaten Nehemiah's life. As he normally did, Nehemiah called out to God, stood his ground, and relentlessly continued the work. Hear Nehemiah's own words about this last-ditch effort to stop him and the work: *"They were just trying to intimidate us, imagining that they could discourage us and stop the work. So I continued the work with even greater determination"* (Neh. 6:9 NLT).

11. Mission accomplished (Perseverance). Nehemiah 6:15-16 says, *"So on October 2 the wall was finished—just fifty-two days after we had begun. When our enemies and the surrounding* *nations heard about it, they were frightened and humiliated. They realized that this work had been done with help of our God"* (NLT). It is so important to stay focused and keep moving forward in what God has given you to do. Refuse to back off or be intimidated. *Stand your ground and be courageous because the Lord your God is with you.*

QUESTIONS FOR THE HEART

1. Have you ever served someone else's vision?

2. Do you have a vision for what you are doing right now? Explain.

3. Why is it important for you to wait for God to raise you up?

4. Can you remember a time when you jumped the gun and did not wait for God? What was the result? What did you learn?

5. Are you struggling to wait for God's perfect timing for your life and ministry?

6. When you think about the next five or ten years, what do you see?

7. Are you "all in" where you are right now?

FOURTEEN
RUN "YOUR" RACE

"Courage doesn't always roar. Sometimes courage is the quiet voice at the end of the day saying 'I will try again tomorrow.'" — Mary Anne Radmacher

THE BIBLE LIKENS the Christian life to being in a race. Unfortunately, many do not even get to the starting line, while others run for a while and then quit when it gets hard. Still others press on regardless of the challenges and obstacles they face, determined to make it to the finish line. Which describes you? Have you made it to the starting blocks? Have you started running but are tired and worn out? Have you found your "sweet spot" or "second wind" and are you running strong for the finish line?

Hebrews 12:1-3 says: *"Therefore, since we are surrounded by such a great cloud of witnesses, let us throw off everything that hinders and the sin that so easily entangles.* **And let us run with perseverance the race marked out for us**, *fixing our eyes on Jesus, the pioneer and perfecter of faith. For the joy set before him he endured the cross, scorning its shame, and sat down at the right hand of the throne of God. Consider him who endured such opposition from sinners, so that you will not grow weary and lose heart"* (NIV emphasis added).

The writer of Hebrews tells us to throw off everything that hinders and **run the race marked out for you**. Find your lane and stay in it. Get rid of anything that hinders you from running your race. Can you imagine running a marathon with a sleeping bag, backpack, and a tent? Metaphorically speaking, that is what we sometimes do in our life and ministry. Some of you are struggling to run your race with so much baggage that it's like dragging a donkey behind you.

When you grow weary and want to quit (you will), think about what Jesus went through and let it inspire you to keep going. We all falter at times and feel like we want to quit running the race. Falling down is not the problem, but getting back up is. The crowd of witnesses Hebrews describes is so important because we are reminded that we are not alone and many are rooting us on. Ever notice how athletic teams do so much better in front of their home crowd rooting and cheering them on? There is nothing like knowing that God Himself and others are cheering for you. Who is cheering you on?

In life and ministry when you find yourself in what seems like an endless dark tunnel with no signs of light at the end, remember that Jesus is not at the end hoping you make it through—He is with you right now in that tunnel to take you to the finish line.

RUN WITH PERSEVERANCE

It is so important when you are in a race that you pre-determine to finish before you start. It's not, "I am trying this Jesus thing and will see how it goes," or "I'm going to such-and-such city to see if I can stir up a church plant." If you say *yes* to Jesus and His plan for your life, you go all in regardless of circumstances. I have seen some church planters who go to a city with high hopes and dreams, but when it doesn't go great right away and they are struggling, they give up, shake off the dust, and move on to another place where they can be "more successful."

I remember Jay Pathak, who is presently the national director of Vineyard USA, when he moved to Colorado to plant a new church. Jay and his wife Danielle did not move to Arvada to see if things "might work out." They became convinced God was calling them to Arvada, Colorado, to plant a church. And they went all in from day one. There were no pre-conditions as it was simply a matter of obedience to what they believed God was saying to them.

That is what got them through the hard times. I know firsthand that the first few years were really hard and challenging for him and Danielle, but they refused to give up and go back to Ohio. At one point, most of his church planting team who joined them at the beginning had left and the church was struggling. At that point, Jay and Danielle made some mid-course corrections and the church began to thrive and grow. This is such a powerful example of what conviction and perseverance can produce. I think this is what Paul had in mind in *Galatians 6:9*: *"Let us not become weary in doing good, for at the proper time we will reap a harvest **if we do not give up***" (NIV emphasis added). And today, the Pathaks are reaping an incredible harvest as the church has grown, launched multiple campuses, and are impacting their city and beyond—all because they refused to give up but stayed the course and continue to run the race God marked out for them.

I ran cross country in college (not well), and it never worked to have a "see-how-it-goes" attitude. Whenever you hit the wall in practice or during a race, there was always a temptation to quit. One time in one of my earlier races, I did just that. I stopped running and quit a race, which was demoralizing and something I would never forget. I decided that day that I would never quit ever again no matter the circumstances, even if I had to crawl across the finish line. And I never quit again and had my best finish in our final meet of the year. I also made Jesus a similar promise that no matter what state or condition I am in, I am going to finish the race He has marked out for me. So much of what God accomplished in my life has occurred simply because I refused to quit when it got hard.

PEOPLE WHO REFUSED TO QUIT

Kurt Warner is a great example of incredible perseverance and determination. Believe it or not, Kurt Warner could've been that guy bagging your groceries if you lived in Iowa. He played football at the University of Northern Iowa with his sights set on the NFL, but he went unselected in the 1994 NFL draft. He was later cut from the Green Bay Packers as the fourth-string quarterback before the start of the season. Discouraged, Kurt returned home and took a job stocking shelves at a grocery store, making just $5.50 an hour. Yes, everything looked pretty hopeless, but his dream didn't end in that grocery store in Iowa. He had a short stint in the Arena Football League before finally getting his chance to play in the NFL in 1998, a surprising turn of events after being told over and over again that he wasn't good enough to be an NFL quarterback.

It wasn't until the Arizona Cardinals took a chance on him that Warner showed he wasn't finished. After finally being given an opportunity to start, Warner had one of his best seasons in 1998. He was second in the NFL with 4,583 yards, which happened to be the second-best yardage output of his entire career in a single season. Warner then went on to play twelve seasons in the NFL. He was twice named the NFL's Most Valuable Player and in 2000 led the St. Louis Rams to a Super Bowl victory. He was subsequently named the Super Bowl MVP and eventually inducted into the Pro Football Hall of Fame in 2017. Not bad for a guy who used to bag groceries for minimum wage but refused to give up on his dreams. Warner once told a reporter, "Your circumstances don't have to be what defines you; your circumstances don't have to be what shapes the final narrative of your life."

Michael Jordan is known around the world as the greatest basketball player to ever play the game (some might argue LeBron James or?). However, what many people might not know about Michael Jordan is that he tried out for his high school's varsity basketball team during his sophomore year and failed to make the cut after being deemed too short to ever play at such a level. Unfazed and determined to press on, he dedicated himself and trained nonstop until he was able to earn a spot on the varsity roster. It was through this perseverance in the face of adversity that he eventually went on to achieve NBA superstardom. "I've missed more than 9,000 shots in my career," Jordan said. "I've lost almost 300 games. Twenty-six times, I've been trusted to take the game-winning shot and missed. I've failed over and over and over again in my life. And that is why I succeed."

Helen Keller became deaf and blind at 19 months due to a serious illness. On September 14, 1964, President Lyndon B. Johnson awarded her the Presidential Medal of Freedom, one of the United States' two highest civilian honors. In 1965 she was elected to the National Women's Hall of Fame at the New York World's Fair. Later, she became the first deaf and blind person to obtain a university degree—but she didn't stop there. She later became a published writer, collaborated with the American Foundation for the Blind, and promoted and worked actively to fight for women's suffrage and workers' rights. Keller showed us that even in the particular and challenging times she lived in, making sure that people with different abilities could live a decent life was important to her. She was an example of what it means to persevere and always work hard to improve yourself for the benefit of others.

Walt Disney was fired from a local newspaper as a young man after his boss told him that he lacked creativity. After his animation company failed, he was barely able to pay his bills and even ate dog food to survive. With his last few dollars, Disney made his way to Hollywood to try and make it big, but he struggled at first. He was told the Mickey Mouse cartoon character was a bad idea and doomed to fail. He faced constant rejection and seemed destined to never succeed. But Disney refused to quit and persisted as he went on to grow the largest entertainment company in the world with amusement parks and feature films. And today he's remembered as a creative genius. "In bad times and in good, I've never lost my sense of zest for life," Disney said. "First, think. Second, believe. Third, dream. And finally, dare. Everyone falls down. Getting back up is how you learn how to walk. The difference between winning and losing is most often not quitting."

These stories remind me of the words from the apostle Paul's letter to the Philippian church. Context is so important here as Paul is writing from a Roman prison, not knowing his fate. He wrote:

> *"I don't mean to say that I have already achieved these things or that I have already reached perfection. But I press on to possess that perfection for which Christ Jesus first possessed me. No, dear brothers and sisters, I have not achieved it, but I focus on this one thing: Forgetting the past and looking forward to what lies ahead, I press on to reach the end of the race and receive the heavenly prize for which God, through Christ Jesus, is calling us"* (Phil. 3:12-14 *NLT*).

Paul acknowledged that there is more to learn and that he was still a long way from being perfect. But he was relentless and focused on forgetting the past and looking to what was in front of him. He wanted to press on to reach the end of the race and receive the heavenly prize. He was in it to win it. What a great example for us today as we face the issues of our lives. For some of you, God wants to break your rearview mirror to stop you from always looking back. (Remember Lot's wife?) God is not behind you—he is out in front of you leading the way forward. You have no grace for the past, only for the moment you are in right now.

DOWN BUT NOT OUT!

In life it's not how many times you get knocked down but how many times you get back up. Paul tells it like it is as he describes the challenges we face in 2 Corinthians 4:9-10,16:

"We are hard pressed on every side, but not crushed; perplexed, but not in despair; persecuted, but not abandoned; struck down, but not destroyed. We always carry around in our body the death of Jesus, so that the life of Jesus may also be revealed in our body. Therefore we do not lose heart. Though outwardly we are wasting away, yet inwardly we are being renewed day by day" (NIV).

When you get knocked down, the key question is whether or not you will get back up. When (not if) you fall down, get up and start running again. Of course, we all have moments when we feel like we can't go on and become tempted to give up. Anybody who has experienced any level of success has overcome and faced failures, disappointments, and roadblocks. The difference is whether you give up and allow them to stop you from pursuing your dreams or use them to propel you on. Quitting seems easy when our situation gets hard, but the regret that comes with it is so much worse.

I broke three ribs in a football game early in my senior year which was devastating, but I had a decision to make: Would I give up on ever playing football again because of the fear of getting hurt, or would I do the work to get back in there and play? After my ribs healed, I eventually got my starting linebacker position back and started the last three games including two playoff games. And even though it cost me All League honors, I refused to let my broken ribs have the last word. Paul knew what it was like to get knocked down, but he got back up over and over again and refused to let his struggles have the final word.

Winston Churchill, who overcame personal disabilities to courageously lead England during their darkest times in World War II, remained undaunted by his circumstances. "Never give in," Churchill famously said. "Never, never, never, never—in nothing, great or small, large or petty—never give in, except to your convictions of honor and good sense. Success is not final, failure is not fatal: it is the courage to continue that counts."

Churchill served as an inspiration to an entire nation under assault from Nazi Germany. That "never give up" attitude became the rallying cry that allowed the people of England to endure great hardship and trepidation. This is what leaders do under adversity and great pressure. They rise up and inspire people to overcome and refuse to give up and therefore experience great victories.

KEEP LEARNING AND GROWING

If you are going to finish your race, it is imperative that you keep learning and growing. Peter Drucker, one of the most influential management experts, wrote, "We now accept the fact that learning is a lifelong process of keeping abreast of change. And the most pressing task is to teach people how to learn."

The apostle Paul writes in Philippians 1:9: *"I pray that your love will overflow more and more, and that you will **keep on growing in knowledge and understanding**"* (NLT). Your whole life is a learning journey in every area of life if you embrace it. Those who finish are those who keep growing and don't stagnate. Just because you graduate and get a degree does not mean your learning is over. On the contrary, it has really just begun.

It's important to all see all of life as your tutor and learn from everyone you can. Some people are book smart and others are street smart—why not be both? Sometimes you need to get your head out of the books and get out in the real world and get some dirt on you. Life's biggest lessons come from not only your successes but also your failures. I love telling young leaders to go make some good mistakes but don't make the same ones!

I have a reputation of being a tenacious learner. As our church hit various barriers, I continually traveled to churches that were one or two steps ahead of where we were to learn everything I could. I also read everything I could get my hands on that dealt with the issues I was facing personally and also in my leadership. My encouragement to you is not only to keep growing, but be tenacious in your pursuit to learn more about how to be a better leader. Go all out and be relentless and learn from everyone you can.

BACK TO SCHOOL

John Wimber was a great example to me about being a lifelong learner. Even after being a reputable church growth consultant, leading a global movement and doing leadership and renewal conferences all over the world, at the age of 60 he was still taking leadership classes at Fuller Seminary where he himself had also taught. Who does that? I'll tell you who—someone who has a huge desire to grow and be the best they can be and refuses to stagnate. I once asked John why he did this and he simply said, "Rick, I want to be a better leader." Now that is someone you can follow—and I did. John was willing to learn from anybody and viewed every encounter as an opportunity to grow. Even when his adversaries would wrongfully come against him, John would always default to this perspective: "God, what do You want to teach me? And what can I learn from this?"

It's hard to lead people beyond where you are, and I have found that to be true. In the early days of our Colorado church plant there were numerous leaders who were drawn to us but over time, as I grew as a leader, so did the quality of those who came our way. Longevity for me has always been tied to whether or not I would keep learning and growing as a person. To lead a church for thirty-seven years required that I keep learning and reinventing myself over and over again. I have also noticed that many leaders grow a lot at the beginning but stall out over time. For me choosing to continue to grow got very tiring. At times I would cry out, "I don't want to go to the next level; it's too hard!" But if our church was to be what it needed to be, then I needed to grow as well. Reflecting over those moments in my journey, I recognize a direct correlation between my personal growth and our church growth. It's important to never see yourself as arriving or "topping" out. The apostle Paul never saw himself as arriving but instead was a lifelong learner to the very end.

Even as you recognize the need to keep growing, understand there is always a next level for every leader. Continually challenge yourself and take steps to move beyond where you are to where you need to be. A few years ago I decided to tackle some very intense topics that some leaders across the country were a bit hesitant to deal with. I spent a year each studying the LGBTQ+ and women in leadership issues from all sides and found it important and helpful. It took plenty of work but was worth it as I came to my own conclusions that I mostly still hold to this day. I could have told myself that it wasn't worth the effort since I am in my sixties and don't have time to learn about all this stuff. But I would have been wrong. Chances are, your theology will change and morph over time. There are some beliefs I was sure of in my younger days that I no longer hold to today. Give yourself room to explore and grow in your theological understanding.

RELYING ON THE HOLY SPIRIT

You need the presence and the power of the Holy Spirit operating in *and* through your life to run your race. When Jesus said, *"Apart from me you can do nothing"* (John 15:5 NIV), He meant it. Self-effort never accomplishes the work of God.

Galatians 3:3 says, *"How foolish can you be? After starting your new lives in the Spirit, why are you now trying to become perfect by your own human effort?"* (NLT). There are two issues in play here. One is that we start with doing everything we can do—and when we hit the wall, we then turn to the Holy Spirit for His strength and power. On the other hand, it's easy to start with a reliance on God's Spirit and then you take over from there and are surprised when nothing seems to be working. Both of these leave us wanting.

What we do starts with the Holy Spirit, continues with the Holy Spirit, and finishes with the Holy Spirit. You will not accomplish anything that is meaningful without relying on the Holy Spirit.

PROCLAMATION *AND* DEMONSTRATION

The apostle Paul was a very educated and gifted leader but made it clear that he did not rely on his gifting but on the Holy Spirit. He also recognized that words, words and more words were not enough. In 1 Corinthians 2:4, the apostle Paul writes, *"My message and my preaching were not with wise and persuasive words, but with a demonstration of the Spirit's power, so that your faith might not rest on human wisdom, but on God's power"* (NIV). Paul's reliance was on the Spirit's power rather than his own. Like Zechariah spoke about, *"... 'Not by might, nor by power, but by my Spirit,' says the Lord Almighty"* (Zech. 4:6 NIV).

We need the proclamation of the gospel but also a demonstration of the Spirit's power. In Acts 1:8, Jesus says, *"But you will receive power when the Holy Spirit comes on you; and you will be my witnesses in Jerusalem, and in all Judea and Samaria, and to the ends of the earth"* (NIV). Before Jesus ascended into heaven He told His disciples to wait in Jerusalem until the Holy Spirit would be poured out upon them. And when it happened, they were transformed and empowered to share the gospel with the whole world like Jesus told them. Without the power of the Holy Spirit, we will not accomplish what God has called us to do. If you are going to be effective in ministry, you absolutely need a demonstration of the Spirit's power. Signs, wonders and miracles are part of the package.

Diane Leman's Miracle Story

When facing impossible situations, do you run to God in hopeful desperation or turn away from Him in bitter disappointment?

"I'm very sorry, Mrs. Leman," said the sober-faced doctor as I sat nervously facing him. "Your test results have revealed that it is going to be nearly impossible for you and your husband ever to conceive your own child. There are too many complications. Please

pursue adoption if you want a family. I've done all I can to help you."

Impossible? The word caused my heart to shatter into a million pieces right along with my lifelong dream of giving birth to a child. After three long years of medical intervention and many dollars spent, I knew I had a choice. I could run to God in hopeful desperation or turn away in bitter disappointment. But, I needed a miracle, and the faith in which I was raised and was now an active member since my marriage five years ago, taught me that miracles had ceased. I was so tempted to harden my heart in hopeless resignation to this God—a God who no longer worked miracles for those facing impossible situations. But my desire overcame my disappointment and I ran to God, and by His amazing grace, I ran right into the Holy Spirit. I had never really heard of the Holy Spirit, although I was a born-again believer in Jesus! I experienced a glorious baptism in the Holy Spirit and my eyes were opened to the truth of Luke 1:37: "For nothing will be impossible with God." As the Holy Spirit continued to reveal that Jesus is still doing miracles, He worked faith in my heart.

Fifteen months after trusting Jesus for the impossible, my doctor declared I was pregnant and that it was indeed a miracle! This changed the entire trajectory of my life. My husband and I left our professional careers and planted a church where we have continued for over forty years to boldly proclaim that God is a God of the impossible and that Jesus is still doing miracles. We have faced many impossible situations in our own lives and in the lives of those we lead and love.

It is always our humble privilege to pray with others and to encourage each to run to God in hopeful desperation and not run from Him in bitter disappointment. I have witnessed God bring healing to hundreds of infertile couples as we give away what He has so graciously given us—a love for the Holy Spirit and faith that with God, nothing is impossible. So young leaders, regardless of whatever issues you will face in your life, remember God is a

God of miracles and you can trust Him for what seems impossible!

Dianne Leman, speaker, author, pastor

BE FILLED AGAIN AND AGAIN!

Paul also made it clear in writing to the Ephesians the importance of being "filled with the Holy Spirit." The grammar in that text suggests that it actually could be translated, "keep on being filled with the Holy Spirit." Being filled with the Holy Spirit is a recurring and ongoing experience. And interestingly enough, those same disciples who were filled with the Holy Spirit in Acts 2 are filled again in Acts 4. You need to be filled with the Spirit over and over again. Ask God to pour out His Spirit and fill you to overflowing. And out of that overflow, you have life to give to those around you. It's a great prayer anytime but especially to start your day.

In leading our church, I continually asked God to fill us with the Holy Spirit. Two of my favorite simple prayers include, "Come, Holy Spirit" and "More, Lord." Simple, yet so powerful. "Come, Holy Spirit" means welcoming the Holy Spirit. It does not mean He isn't there, but it is asking Him to manifest His presence among us. "More, Lord" is our cry for all that God has for us. "Lord, fill me to overflowing, I want more of you and all that you have for me." More love and more power!

Young leader, the Holy Spirit is your friend and is God's gift to you as you navigate your way through this life. Welcome Him into the now of your life and watch what happens. Three helpful resources are, *Hello Holy Spirit: God's Gift of Live-In Help!* by Dianne Leman, *When the Spirit Comes in Power* by John White and *Surprised by the Power of the Spirit* by Jack Deere.

THE FAITHFULNESS OF GOD

> *"The one who calls you is faithful, and he will do it"* (1 Thess. 5:24 NIV).

God is able to do above and beyond anything we can ask or think. The Bible declares over and over that God is faithful. It is God's faithfulness that sustains you and launches you into the adventure of His kingdom. Will you trust Him with your life, ministry and your future? When you see how God has been faithful to previous generations, you can be assured that He will again be faithful to you, for that is who He is! He is the same yesterday, today, and forever.

I leave you with this final quote from Lou Engle: "*There are moments in history when a door for massive change opens, and great revolutions for good or evil spring up in the vacuum created by these openings. In these divine moments key men and women and even entire generations risk everything to become the hinge of history, the pivotal point that determines which way the door will swing.*"

Will you be one of those men or women who risk everything to become the hinge of history for the glory of God? If you dare to say *yes*, God is faithful and **He will do it!**

QUESTIONS FOR THE HEART

1. Have you pre-determined to finish your race?

2. Do you believe that with God all things are possible? Give an example of this belief as it has been worked out in your life.

3. How have you experienced the Holy Spirit working in your life?

4. What do you need in order to run and finish your race?

5. Is there an area of ministry or your personal life where you have hit the wall? Have you reached out for help?

6. Do you have baggage that makes you hesitant to embrace the ministry of the Holy Spirit?

7. What do you need to trust God for right now?

NOTES

10. DON'T SACRIFICE YOUR LIFE (OR FAMILY) ON THE ALTAR OF MINISTRY

1. Jones, Peter, dir. *Ozzie & Harriet: The Adventures of America's Favorite Family*. 1998; New York, NY: A&E Networks, 1998.
2. *Merriam-Webster.com Dictionary*, s.v. "holy," accessed April 5, 2023, https://www.merriam-webster.com/dictionary/holy.

11. KEEP SHORT ACCOUNTS

1. Wimber, John. 1992. "Position Paper: Why I Respond to Criticism." *Vineyard USA*. https://vineyardusa.org/position-paper-why-i-respond-to-criticism/.

ABOUT THE AUTHOR

For seven years, prior to moving to Colorado, Rick was bi-vocational in a small California community leading a church of fifty to sixty people while teaching special Education, coaching various high school sports and eventually starting and becoming a principal of a new alternative high school. He and his wife Becky moved to Colorado in 1982 to start a second church and again, Rick found himself bi-vocational for two years as the church grew and doubled from 100 to 200, then 400 and then 800 in the first four years. At one point, they had over 70 small groups, a large staff and over 2,000 in attendance. In addition, three campuses/satellites were launched of which two were later released to be autonomous churches.

Rick served on the National Board of the Vineyard Movement and led various task forces, including youth, young adults and evangelism while functioning as a regional overseer to over forty churches for the Rocky Mountain Region. He and Becky traveled to over thirty countries sharing stories of redemption and training pastors and leaders in Europe, Eastern Europe, New Zealand, Australia and more recently, the Middle East. Along the way Rick also helped plant or send pastors to over 35 churches. Rick also experienced plenty of failure along the way, some quite devastating. In 2019, Rick led a healthy transition of the church he had spent 37 years pastoring to a new lead pastor who was half his age. Then, unexpectedly, Rick and Becky moved to California's Central Coast to help rescue an imploding church and, also unexpectedly, became the interim lead pastors during the Covid-

19 pandemic for two years. They are still living in San Luis Obispo, and they lead a nonprofit ministry called Generation Now and the Global 4/14 Window Movement (414movement.com).

Ministry Biography and Background

- Married to Becky Olmstead since 1979.
- Twin boys Geoff and Greg.
- Currently living in San Luis Obispo, California.
- Graduated from Vanguard University with a BA in Psychology/Social Science and a minor in Bible.
- MA from California State University, Bakersfield in Education/Counseling.
- Held Secondary California Teaching Credentials in Counseling, Special Education and Social Sciences and also holds a lifetime teaching credential from California Community Colleges.
- Served 20 years as a volunteer police chaplain in Fort Collins, CO, while pastoring the Vineyard Church of the Rockies for 37 years.

Made in the USA
Columbia, SC
15 March 2025